ZHOU DAGUAN

A RECORD OF CAM.

THE LAND AND ITS PEOPLE

ZHOU DAGUAN

A RECORD OF CAMBODIA
THE LAND AND ITS PEOPLE

Translated with an Introduction and Notes by
PETER HARRIS

Foreword by
DAVID CHANDLER

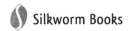 Silkworm Books

FOR VICKY WITH LOVE

ISBN: 978-974-9511-24-4

First published by Silkworm Books in 2007
Silkworm Books
430/58 Soi Ratchaphruek, M. 7, T. Mae Hia, A. Mueang Chiang Mai, Thailand 50100
info@silkwormbooks.com
www.silkwormbooks.com

Typeset in Janson Pro 11 pt. by Silk Type

Printed and bound in the United States by Lightning Source

CONTENTS

A RECORD OF CAMBODIA: THE LAND AND ITS PEOPLE

FOREWORD

IN AUGUST 1296, Zhou Daguan (c. 1270–c. 1350), a native of Wenzhou, a coastal city south of Shanghai, arrived at Yasodharapura, the capital of Cambodia, as part of an official delegation sent by the Chinese Emperor Temür (r. 1294–1307).

Zhou stayed at Yasodharapura (which we know today as "Angkor") for eleven months. When he returned home he composed *A Record of Cambodia—The Land and Its People*, perhaps as part of an official report. We know almost nothing of his subsequent career. Moreover, as Peter Harris reminds us in the introduction to his fresh and absorbing translation, what has come down to us may well be less than half of what Zhou originally wrote.

Even in its truncated form, *A Record of Cambodia—The Land and Its People* is the only surviving eyewitness account of daily life at Angkor. Written by an alert young foreigner with a wide range of interests, Zhou's memoir has immense historical value. In Harris' deft, accessible translation, it is also fun to read.

Zhou's memoir was first translated into French in 1819, but it did not have much impact until 1902, when it was retranslated into French by Paul Pelliot (1878–1945). By the time Pelliot's version appeared, Angkor had been "discovered" by the French and France had established its protectorate over Cambodia. Scholars of Cambodia were quick to recognize the value of Pelliot's excellent translation. In his old age, Pelliot returned to Zhou's memoir, and a partly revised translation appeared in 1951. This posthumous text, in turn, formed the basis for English-language translations that were published in recent years.

It has been over half a century, in other words, since Zhou's original text has been revisited and over a century since it has been translated in full into a European language. In the meantime, great advances have been made in scholarship about Angkor and about thirteenth-century China. In his helpful introduction and his copious notes Harris locates Zhou's memoir in the context of thirteenth-century Chinese literature and history, and places Zhou's remarks about Cambodia in the context of what we know about the kingdom from a range of other sources.

Until the 1970s, archaeological work at Angkor concentrated on the temples, and writings about the kingdom stressed the activities of priests, princes, and kings; the development of artistic styles; and what can be gleaned from statuary and inscriptions about Cambodian governance and religion. What we know about everyday life, aside from Zhou's account, came largely from the teeming bas-reliefs of the Bayon and, to a lesser extent, those of Angkor Wat. From a scholarly point of view, and for visitors who now number more than a million a year, Yasodharapura was a ruined, empty city, with many of its temples restored but with its people missing.

In the mid-1970s, archaeology came to a halt for over twenty years as Cambodia suffered from civil war, aerial bombardment, and the Khmer Rouge regime, as well as more than a decade of international isolation. In the mid-1990s, when archeology revived in Cambodia, many archaeologists began to concentrate on studying Yasodharapura not only from the "top" but also as a thriving, low density city which contained in its heyday perhaps as many as six hundred thousand people. Recent scholarly work has filled the Angkorian landscape with canals, roads, villages, and inhabitants. The new popularizing emphasis fits neatly with Zhou's account, which shows us thirteenth-century

Yasodharapura as a lived-in, monumental city, crowded with princes, priests, merchants, slaves, travelers, and appealingly ordinary people.

Peter Harris first visited Angkor in 1969, a year before he graduated from Oxford with first-class honors in Chinese. Since then, he has had a varied and exciting career as a scholar, a teacher, an NGO official, and a writer and producer for the BBC. Over the years, he has lived and worked in China, Indonesia, New Zealand, India, and Cambodia, where in 2005–2006 he directed a multi-million dollar USAID-sponsored program concerned with human rights and governance. His scholarly turn of mind, his flair for writing, and his long exposure to Asia have ideally suited him to bridge the gap between Zhou's occasionally elusive classical Chinese and the mysteries of Angkor on the one hand and, on the other, the everyday people, events, and culture that Zhou so vividly brings to life.

In his edition of Zhou Daguan's *A Record of Cambodia—The Land and Its People*, Peter Harris has given a new generation of readers a masterly version of Zhou's timeless and fascinating account that scholars of Cambodia are sure to relish and visitors to Angkor are sure to enjoy.

David Chandler

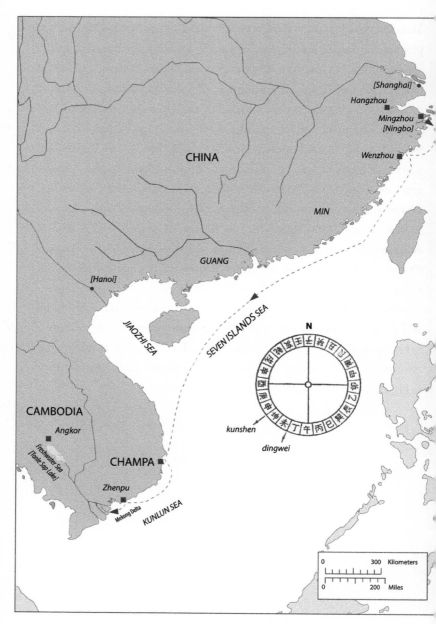

Map of Zhou Daguan's outward route

PREFACE

I FIRST VISITED Angkor in June 1969, as a student of Chinese en route from Hong Kong to London. Its mysterious buildings stood silently in the surrounding forest, and were almost completely deserted. I understood almost nothing about what I was looking at. Nor did I have ready access to a guidebook. There were none of the children selling books, cards, cold drinks, and trinkets, let alone the regiment of glamorous hotels with their hooded snakes and Jayavarman statuary that now fill the Siem Reap skyline.

Like most people, I was captivated by the stillness and timelessness of Angkor. But once home I was soon distracted by other interests. I went back to Cambodia in 1981–1982 as the Oxfam Field Director in Phnom Penh, but Angkor was closed to visitors. Pol Pot's forces were said to be billeted in some of the buildings, and there were dark stories about the war damage being done to them. (Nothing, it turned out, compared to the damage done by art thieves since then.) But I never got closer than Kampong Thom along a road—Route 6—that, like much of the country, was in ruinous condition. My time with Oxfam in Cambodia was brief, and again, I soon became involved in work elsewhere. The buildings of Angkor stayed in the back of my mind as a place to return to one day. But for the next two decades I did not give them much thought.

Then in 2004 my wife Vicky and I visited our old friend Margo Picken, who was working with the UN in Phnom Penh. One day she picked up one of the English versions of Zhou Daguan's text and flourished it in the air. There was a need for an English translation from the original Chinese, she said. Why didn't I do it?

Rashly, I agreed. After all, it was only a short book. Moreover by this time I had visited Angkor a second time and rediscovered its delights. I soon found out, however, that even with the help of the Chinese scholar Xia Nai's annotated edition, the work was going to take time. In the end it took many months. Even now I have hardly begun to explore the many textual, linguistic, historical, and artistic avenues that a study of Zhou's work opens up.

My thanks go to Margo Picken, then, for giving me the idea of doing the translation, and for being a steady source of encouragement. Many others have offered help and advice as well. Duncan Campbell, the Chinese classicist at Victoria University of Wellington, New Zealand, brought his wide-ranging knowledge and insights to bear on my rendering of the text and on materials relating to it. Helen Ibbitson Jessup found time off from her work as one of Cambodia's leading art historians to take an enthusiastic interest. David Chandler at Monash University, whose very readable account of Cambodian history I found of immense help in the early stages of my work, reacted positively to my work and was kind enough to offer to write a foreword. He was also the one who put me in touch with Silkworm Books. Iulian Circo generously gave up his time to roam Angkor with his customary energy and a panoply of photographic equipment, and provided me with many new photos to draw on.

Igor de Rachewiltz at the Australian National University in Canberra offered his time and his unrivalled knowledge of Yuan dynasty names. Hugh Blackstock at Victoria University of Wellington provided expert assistance in making the two maps. Mai Nguyen-Pham wielded her fine brush for the title calligraphy. Roger and Judith Peren, Philip Morrison, Kent Davis, Reed Aeschliman, Sin Kim Sean,

Zheng Hong, Li Xin and Miyako Armitage helped with contacts and materials. Nothing was too hard to locate for Naomi Eisenthal and her colleagues at Victoria University library. I am grateful to them all for their support.

Trasvin Jittidecharak, Publisher and Director of Silkworm Books, her Senior Editor Susan Offner, and the Silkworm team have been unfailingly patient and professional. Their outside editor Edwin Zehner made a number of helpful suggestions and spotted various errors that should never have been there. Needless to say the mistakes that remain are my responsibility.

Finally, I want to say a very special thank you to my wife Vicky and my three children Max, Ben, and Alexis. Max, Ben, and Alexis have all gone out of their way to visit Angkor and explore it for themselves. I hope they find a chance to revisit its many delights sometime later in life. Vicky's interest and encouragement have been essential to seeing this work through to completion, as they have been in so many other ways.

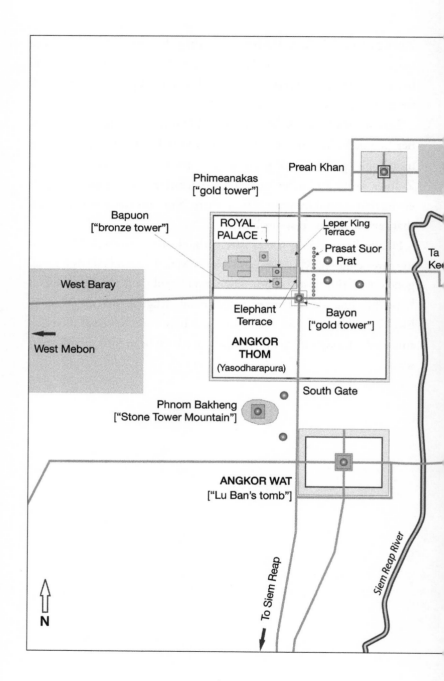

Preah Khan

Phimeanakas ["gold tower"]

Bapuon ["bronze tower"]

ROYAL PALACE

Leper King Terrace

Prasat Suor Prat

Ta Ke

West Baray

West Mebon

Elephant Terrace

Bayon ["gold tower"]

ANGKOR THOM (Yasodharapura)

South Gate

Phnom Bakheng ["Stone Tower Mountain"]

ANGKOR WAT ["Lu Ban's tomb"]

To Siem Reap

Siem Reap River

N

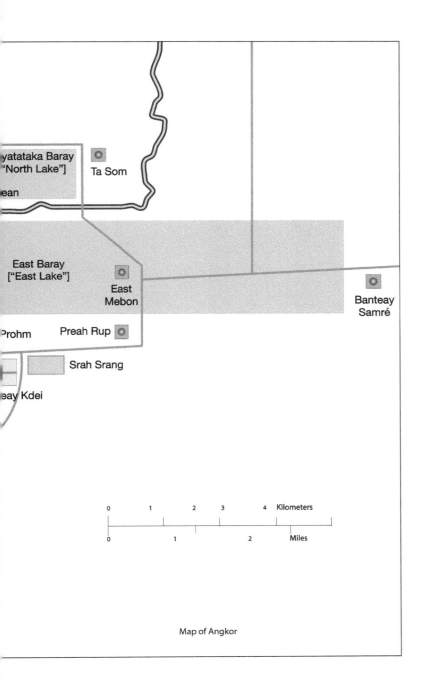

yatataka Baray
["North Lake"]

ean

Ta Som

East Baray
["East Lake"]

East
Mebon

Banteay
Samré

Prohm

Preah Rup

Srah Srang

eay Kdei

| 0 | 1 | 2 | 3 | 4 | Kilometers |

| 0 | 1 | 2 | Miles |

Map of Angkor

Fig. 1. The south gate of Angkor Thom from the outside, showing three of its four heads, and the central spire where the fifth head described by Zhou would have been.

Fig. 2. Deities holding a snake or naga on the west side of the south gate of Angkor Thom, "all pulling at the snake with their hands . . . as if they are preventing it from escaping" (chapter 1). The snake in their hands has seven heads, rather than the nine that Zhou describes.

Fig. 3. Demons, some with recently restored heads, pulling at a snake on the east side of the south gate of Angkor Thom.

Fig. 4. A view of the moat around Angkor Thom, parts of it now dry, with the demons to the east of the south gate in the distance.

Fig. 5. Tiered heads of five or more heads were common features of sculpture seen in Angkor in Zhou's time. This photo shows an undated sculpture with many heads, clearly not in its original location, now located near the south gate of Angkor Thom.

Fig. 6. Many of the extant naga at Angkor, including those at the gateways to Angkor Thom, have seven heads. This photo shows the unusual sight of a nine-headed naga, surmounted by a garuda (mythical bird), at Banteay Kdei. It raises a question about Zhou's description of the nine-headed naga at the gateways to Angkor Thom. Was he mistaken, or did they have more heads in 1296–97 than they have now?

Fig. 7. "The inside of the walls are built like a slope" (chapter 1). The gradual slope inside the walls, contrasting with the vertical drop on the outside, is still visible all round the perimeter of Angkor Thom. This photo shows the slope inside the south gate.

Fig. 8. The wall near the south gate of Angkor Thom. "The walls are all made of piled-up stones, and are . . . very tightly packed and firm" (chapter 1).

Fig. 9. Each of the five gates to Angkor Thom is still surmounted by four heads, most of them well preserved. This is the head on the north side of the east gate.

Fig. 10. The causeway leading into Bayon, with two lions, their mouths damaged, and the head of a naga. "To the east . . . [of Bayon] is a golden bridge flanked by two gold lions, one on the left and one on the right" (chapter 1).

Fig. 12. Bakheng: "beyond the south gate is Stone Tower Mountain . . . it is about ten *li* in circumference, and has several hundred stone chambers" (chapter 1).

Fig. 11. A view of the lower part of Bayon. "In the center of the city is a gold tower, flanked by twenty or so stone towers and a hundred or so stone chambers" (chapter 1).

(*Right page*) **Fig. 13.** A view of Bapuon, now undergoing extensive renovation, as the crane shows: "About a *li* north of the gold tower there is a bronze tower. It is even taller than the gold tower, and an exquisite sight" (chapter 1).

Fig. 14. The classic view of Angkor Wat, which Zhou describes as the tomb of the Chinese carpenter Lu Ban. "Lu Ban's tomb is . . . about ten li in circumference, and has several hundred stone chambers" (chapter 1). Why did Zhou say so little about this magnificent structure?

Fig. 15. ". . . men and women . . . wear their hair in a topknot" (chapter 6). From a relief at Angkor Wat.

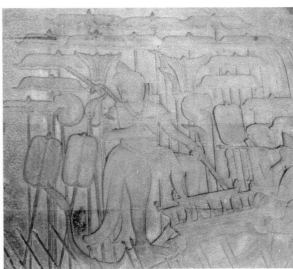

Fig. 16. From the famous bas relief at Angkor Wat showing King Suryavarman II in procession on an elephant with fifteen parasols with floral designs around him. In chapters 3 and 4 Zhou describes and flower patterns were symbols of high rank.

Fig. 17. Phimeanakas, the gold tower in the king's palace. "In the inner palace there is a gold tower, at the summit of which the king sleeps at night. The local people all say that in the tower lives a nine-headed snake spirit which is lord of the earth for the entire country" (chapter 2).

Fig. 18. All that remains of the room at the top of the tower today.

Fig. 19. Four of the "twelve small stone towers [Prasat Suor Prat] on a bank opposite the palace" where, according to Zhou, families settled disputes by lodging disputants until one of them fell ill (chapter 14).

Fig. 20. An entrance gate on the south side of the wall surrounding the palace, leading straight from Bapuon to Phimeanakas.

Fig. 21. A view of the larger of the two tanks or ponds in the northeastern part of the royal palace enclosure. They are all that remains of the palace except Phimeanakas, scattered stones, a small subterranean structure, and the surrounding walls. Was this tank where the Buddha bathing ceremony described in chapter 13 was held?

Fig. 22. The lion and the elephant in the chapels at Neak Pean, which Zhou seems to be describing at the end of chapter 1.

Fig. 23. East Mebon (*left*), where Zhou claims a bronze reclining Buddha was located (chapter 1). Did he confuse this with the bronze reclining Vishnu (*above*) found in West Mebon and now on display in the National Museum in Phnom Penh?

Fig. 24. A small boat with oarsmen and a warrior doing battle. Zhou describes such boats, which he calls pilan, in chapter 32. From a relief at Bayon.

Fig. 25. "There are a great many cows . . . used to haul carts and nothing else" (chapter 24). From a relief at Bayon.

Fig. 26. "Their palanquins are made of pieces of wood that bend in the middle and point upwards at either end . . . [and are] carried by two people" (chapter 31). A woman in a palanquin from a relief at Bayon.

INTRODUCTION

JUST OVER SEVEN centuries ago the trader and adventurer Marco Polo arrived back in Venice after twenty-five years' absence. Legend has it that he was full of stories about his travels in China and other parts of Asia, and about the services he provided to the great khan Khubilai, the founding emperor of the Mongol dynasty then ruling China.

That same year, 1295, a young man by the name of Zhou Daguan made ready to set sail from Mingzhou, a port on the southeast coast of China. Zhou was headed for Cambodia as part of a delegation sent there by Khubilai's grandson Temür, who had come to the imperial throne on the death of his grandfather.

Three years later, while in detention in a Genoese prison, Marco Polo related his memoirs to a fellow prisoner, Rustichello da Pisa, who wrote them down and turned them into a book. The book, known variously as *The Travels* and *The Description of the World*, ran to many editions and many versions, and helped shape Europe's view of China for centuries to come. By this time, Zhou Daguan had returned to China and was writing or preparing to write a book about his experiences in Cambodia. Since the first appearance of his book, *A Record of Cambodia—The Land and Its People (Zhenla fengtu ji)*, it too has been copied, circulated, anthologized, published, and republished. Zhou's book gives us a unique insight into day-to-day life in the state of Angkor during the final years of its glory.[1]

1

In their books the two men come across as having quite different styles. Marco Polo is enthusiastic, wordy, and sometimes highly informative, but his memoirs are often unclear. Sometimes his itineraries are confusing and his stories second-hand. There are doubts about where he actually went, and a few skeptics ask whether he got to China at all. Even if, like me, you believe he did go, you have to ask why there is no mention of him in Chinese records, and why he fails to mention the most obvious things—the Chinese writing system, the Great Wall of China, the bound feet of Chinese women? At the very least, skeptics argue, the many versions of his book that have been handed down to us are amalgams of myth, story, and travelogue.

Zhou Daguan, on the other hand, gives us the impression he can be relied on. In his book—or what is left of it—he tells us how he got to Cambodia, and what he saw there. He gets many of the details about Angkor right (though he gets a few wrong, too). And he persuades us that most of what he tells us he has seen first-hand. It is true that there are some unanswered questions. Why does Zhou never mention a single Cambodian by name? And how come the official Chinese records make no mention of *his* mission, either? On the whole, though, the detail and precision of Zhou's memoirs give them a more dependable air than those of the Venetian.

For centuries Zhou's work has been a major point of reference for Cambodian history. In China it was apparently used in the first official review of Cambodia written after Zhou's death, the account in the official history of the Ming dynasty. It was also later preserved in the monumental eighteenth-century collection of writings compiled by the Manchu emperor Qianlong. Western scholars have drawn on Zhou's descriptions to gain a picture of everyday palace life and protocols, religious practitioners and practices, the role of women and slaves, trade and city life, agriculture, the Chinese in Cambodia, and other aspects of society in Angkor, particularly in Yasodharapura, the capital city at the center of Angkor. In Cambodia itself what Zhou recorded has become part of the history the nation has made for itself. In the late 1970s the murderous Khmer Rouge regime is said to have pushed for four harvests of rice annually because that was the number of harvests the farmers brought in, according to Zhou. Today Zhou's stories and descriptions are learned in schools and recounted by the Cambodian guides who escort the busloads of Korean, Japanese, Chinese, American, German, and other visitors around Angkor every day.

These guides draw on the various guidebooks now available on Angkor, and the guidebooks, in turn, draw on the French translation of Zhou's book that was published in 1902 by the legendary scholar Paul Pelliot. There had only been one translation of the book before Pelliot's, a version in French by Jean-Pierre-Abel Rémusat in 1819. Pelliot's translation superseded that, and has remained unsurpassed ever since, thanks to his language skills and his meticulous, even obsessive concern for detail. (When a student of his once plucked up enough courage to ask the great man why he spent so much of his wonderful talent on such minutiae, Pelliot famously responded, "Ça m'amuse . . . ça m'amuse.") Pelliot died in 1945, before completing the comprehensive notes he planned to provide for Zhou's text. They went no further than the first few hundred words of the text, leaving readers like myself still wanting to know why he had chosen this or that interpretation.

Pelliot's French version has been translated into English more than once, most recently by Michael Smithies in a book published by the Siam Society in 2001 under the title *The Customs of Cambodia*. Smithies takes into consideration some of the variants in the Chinese text that have come to light in recent decades. But he himself acknowledges he does not read Chinese, and his translation inevitably suffers from being two removes from the original. An earlier translation into English by J. Gilman d'Arcy Paul suffers from the same problems, in a more pronounced form.[2]

Taking all this into account, a translation directly into English of Zhou's original literary Chinese text is long overdue. The translation I am offering here will, I hope, be helpful not only to scholars, but also to the increasing number of tourists going to Angkor. Over a million people now visit Cambodia each year, many of them English-speaking, and I can think of no better way of helping them enjoy Angkor than to offer them an accurate English version of what Zhou wrote, an account to read when the sun is too hot for sightseeing.[3]

～ ～

To enjoy the work of a long-dead author it helps to know about his life and times. In Zhou Daguan's case we can recreate a picture of his times, but as far as his life is concerned we know frustratingly little. We cannot even be completely sure of his name, which crops up in more than one version in the centuries after his death. One source calls him Zhou Jianguan rather than Zhou Daguan, while in another he is called Zhou Dake.[4]

Working back from later evidence, we can assume Zhou was born in the second half of the thirteenth century, probably in the 1270s. We know, too, that he came from Yongjia, now a small town near the port city of Wenzhou, but in Zhou's time it was a name often used for Wenzhou itself. The fact that Zhou was a man from the Wenzhou area is in itself quite helpful in giving us some insights into his nature and his outlook on life.

Wenzhou is not a place many people outside China have heard of, but it was—and still is—a bustling port city in southeast China, roughly halfway between present-day Hong Kong and Shanghai. It has a reputation for dynamism and commercial acumen, and was recently described by *The Financial Times* as a bastion of Chinese capitalism.[5] It is a very old city, dating back to the third century if not earlier, making it one of the oldest continuously occupied urban centers in east Asia. From what we know of it, it has always had a kind of frontier spirit. In Zhou's day it was a place for business and foreign trade, manufacture and handicraft, art and entertainment. Like other coastal cities in southeast China it was also a place of many faiths and forms of learning, with Moslems and the occasional Christian mingling with Buddhists, Daoists, and scholars in the Confucian tradition. Zhou himself was evidently inclined toward Buddhism, as were most of his contemporaries, since at one point he refers respectfully to "the spiritual power of the holy Buddha."

Among the Confucian scholars in Wenzhou would have been followers and critics of Zhu Xi (1130–1200), whose family home had been a couple of hundred miles west of Wenzhou as the bird flies. Zhu Xi's syncretic system of thought had overcome a more utilitarian strand of Confucian thinking associated with Wenzhou, and was becoming the new China-wide Confucian orthodoxy, which it would remain until the twentieth century.[6]

The Wenzhou people's sense of local identity would have been reinforced by their use of the Wu dialect or language, which is still spoken in Wenzhou and in other places nearby, including Shanghai. In his book Zhou uses straightforward literary Chinese, but there are words and structures here and there that seem to be influenced by this dialect, as for example when he seems to use the Wenzhou words for a comb and for gooseneck barnacles, a shellfish delicacy.

Songs and stories in the Wu dialect helped make Wenzhou a major center of dramatic performance. In Zhou's time the city was the home of the "southern drama" (*nan xi*), one of its main claims to national fame. Developed in the twelfth century, southern drama was born out of Wu folk opera, perhaps with some Indian influence. Rich in comic and tragic themes, it consisted of plays made up of song, dance, and recitative, accompanied by music using a pentatonic or five-note scale. Most of these plays have since been lost, and only a few, such as "The Story of the Lute," have survived to the present day. Some scholars believe southern drama was the earliest form of Chinese drama. It certainly played a major role in making drama the cultural highlight of the Yuan dynasty, the best stagecraft in the world at that time.[7]

Wenzhou was one of a string of old port cities stretched out along the coast of southeast China.[8] From what is known about them they all seemed to share broadly the same way of life. From north to south these cities were Hangzhou; Mingzhou, known today as Ningbo, where Zhou set out from when he went to Cambodia; Wenzhou itself; Fuzhou, the capital of today's Fujian province; the great trading port of Quanzhou, sometimes known in the West as Zayton; and Guangzhou, sometimes called Canton, the capital of today's province of Guangdong.

These were the main staging posts for the export to southeast Asia and places further afield of a host of goods and products from southern China. They included lacquerware and celadon—green-glaze pottery—from the kilns at Longquan (Dragon Spring), not far from Wenzhou. They also included ceramics from further inland, specifically from the famous kiln complex at Jingdezhen—nowadays billed on tourist websites as "the ceramics metropolis of China"—and from the kilns at Dexing, Anfu, and Dehua. Zhou himself mentions the demand in Cambodia for a range of Chinese goods and products, all of which would have been carried on trading junks from these southern ports. According to Zhou they included gold and silver, colored silks, mercury, cinnabar, paper, sulphur, saltpeter, sandalwood, musk, iron and copper products, pewter ware from up the Yangzi River, combs, needles, umbrellas, glass balls, herbs, hemp and cloth, tung tree oil, and grass mats from Wenzhou's sister port of Mingzhou, which evidently specialized in these prosaic but important items. The most celebrated of these port cities were Hangzhou and Quanzhou, both of which stirred the admiration of foreign visitors and local Chinese alike. Hangzhou had been the capital of the southern Song dynasty until it was captured by Mongol forces in 1276, when Zhou was probably still a small boy. With a population of a million or more, it rivaled Angkor as one of the largest metropolises known to man. In *The Description of the World* Marco Polo calls Hangzhou "without doubt the finest and most splendid city in the world." He describes its many attributes (from first-hand experience, we can only hope), including its great lake and streams, myriad bridges, twelve large markets, wealthy merchants, silk-clad inhabitants, well-drained paved roads, constant flow of carriages, large and numerous public baths, and paper money.[9]

Marco Polo's enthusiasm is shared by several contemporary Chinese writers, including Wu Zimu, the otherwise unknown author of *Gruel Dream (Meng liang lu)*, which tells of a poor farmer dreaming of the splendors of Hangzhou as he waits for his meager bowl of porridge. Its author lovingly describes Hangzhou in all its aspects: its rented houses, hospitals, cemeteries, rice and fish markets, waterway barges loaded with produce, shops, restaurants—he names over four hundred dishes that could be ordered there—taverns, pleasure grounds, tea-houses, courtesans, sex workers, story-tellers, actors, dancers, acrobats, agents, fixers, idlers, beggars, and unemployed. Just to give you a sample of the vivid picture he paints, here is his description of a scene in a Hangzhou restaurant:

> When the clients have chosen where they will sit, chopsticks are handed to them and they are asked what they want to eat. The

people of Hang are extremely difficult to please: this one wants something hot, that one something cold, a third something tepid, a fourth something chilled; one wants cooked food, another raw, another chooses roast, another grill. The orders shouted out by the customers, each making his own choice, are all different, there being sometimes as many as three separate orders at one table. Having received the orders, the waiter goes to the kitchen and sings out the whole list, starting with the first one. . . . When the waiter has come to end of his list, he takes his tray to the stove and then goes off to serve each customer with the dish ordered. He never mixes them up, and if by any unlikely chance he should make a mistake, and the customer complains, the proprietor of the restaurant will launch into a volley of oaths, and will make him stop serving immediately, and may even dismiss him altogether.[10]

Gruel Dream was written in 1274, just two years before Hangzhou was occupied by Mongol troops—or at least by troops loyal to the Mongols, since many of the rank-and-file soldiers were actually Chinese. The troops were commanded by one of Khubilai Khan's most able generals, Sodu, who later led the Mongol thrust into mainland southeast Asia, and who happens to be one of only a handful of people that Zhou mentions by name in his book.

The people of Hangzhou, like the people of Wenzhou, must have trembled as Sodu's forces approached, as the Mongols had a truly fearsome reputation. But in the end the city was not too badly affected. Khubilai was less inclined to order the destruction of subjugated populations than many of his relatives, and his occupation of south China was less brutal than the Mongols' earlier, devastating occupation of the north had been. (A careful assessment by the American scholar F. W. Mote suggests that the population of north China, around 50 to 60 million in the early part of the thirteenth century, decreased by roughly two-thirds between then and 1290, presumably from a combination of death, disease, famine, migration, and lost births. That is a loss of 33 to 40 million people in eighty years or so, a statistic that puts the terrible losses of twentieth-century Europe and Asia in a revealing light.)[11]

Once it was occupied by the Mongols, Hangzhou lost its status as the imperial capital. The capital shifted to Dadu, a new city built by Khubilai Khan on the site of present-day Beijing. Without the emperor and the court, Hangzhou went gradually downhill. Even so it remained a center of trade and the arts and a place of great sophistication for at least as long as Zhou was alive. As such its culture must have been felt in nearby Wenzhou, and would surely have affected Zhou as a young man, and indeed throughout his life. He may well have visited the city, perhaps even when Marco Polo was there, and succumbed to its charms in the same way as the author of *Gruel Dream* did. He certainly had one good opportunity to do so, for when he went to Cambodia in 1296 he set out from Mingzhou, only a hundred miles or so south of Hangzhou—a short enough boat ride for a curious young envoy.

The other outstanding city whose influence Zhou would have felt was Quanzhou, located midway between Zhou's home town of Wenzhou and the southern city of Canton. Known to medieval European travelers as Zayton, Quanzhou had the reputation of being the greatest port in China, perhaps the whole world, and was much admired by visitors from the Mediterranean. The fourteenth-century Florentine priest Giovanni dei Marignolli called it *"portus maris mirabilis, civitas nobis incredibilis"*—"a marvellous seaport, an incredible city to us." The fourteenth-century traveler Ibn Battuta, an Arab born in Tangier, judged it to be the greatest of the five great ports of the world, the others being Calicut and Kulam in India, Soldaia in the Crimea, and Alexandria in Egypt.[12]

Quanzhou was shipyard for the great Chinese trading junks that plied the southern seas. These impressive ships were a feature of maritime life from the late Song dynasty onward, and may originally have been modeled on ships from Java. By the early twelfth century they were, according to one Chinese observer, built "like houses," capable of carrying several hundred men and enough grain rations for a year. Marco Polo has left us with an account of them. The larger ships, he tells us, were provided with thirteen bulkheads or partitions, crews of up to three hundred men, and the capacity to carry very large cargoes—five or six thousand baskets of pepper, for example. Zhou Daguan refers to a junk carrying "two or three thousand honeycombs of beeswax" out of Cambodia, a cargo of comparable size. The ships were propelled by oars and sails, and had two or three smaller boats in attendance. When he went to Cambodia Zhou probably sailed on one of these ships. It seems from what he writes in his general preface that he traveled on a large ship, sailing straight in from the ocean and up the Mekong River as far as Tonle Sap Lake, where he had to change to a smaller vessel.[13]

The ships of Quanzhou were not only for trading. They also served as a navy. When the Moslem superintendent of maritime trade in Quanzhou (which had a sizeable Moslem population) transferred his loyalty from the Song emperor to Khubilai Khan in 1277, Khubilai inherited the Song naval fleet. He used this fleet for one arm of his invasion of Japan in 1281, and for a naval expedition to Java nine years later.

Such, then, were the people Zhou Daguan grew up with—traders, merchants and sailors, broad-minded, outward-looking, well-versed in the affairs of the world, living in a community of like-minded coastal cities, with the former Song capital just to the north of them, and China's greatest port just down the coast. They had been shaken by the Mongol invasion of China, but retained a strong sense of identity, reinforced by their local language and drama, and remained pleasure seekers and bons vivants.

If you are a careful reader of Zhou's book you may recognize his appreciation of good living in his description of the good things to eat in Cambodia. His accounts of the royal court, the grand buildings of the capital, the festivals, women bathing—all these, too, have the air of a man enjoying what he has seen. His love of women (or men), on the other hand, is less in evidence—his comments on matters sexual have a touch of prudery about them. This is not inconsistent with the portrait of Zhou as an urbane Wenzhou man. There was a certain prudishness among men of Zhou's background, and we get a sense of this, too, in what we read.

Getting back to what we know of Zhou's life, the first and only event in it that we are aware of was the official mission to Cambodia and the nearby state of Champa—roughly present-day southern Vietnam—that he was told to join in 1295. The purpose of the mission, Zhou informs us, was to deliver "an imperial edict." Presumably it was charged with proclaiming the accession of Temür as emperor and securing recognition of Mongol suzerainty. It was probably also a kind of mission of peace. Temür was a less aggressive and ambitious man than his grandfather. In pursuit of global domination Khubilai had tried to invade Japan twice, and had sent five military expeditions to mainland southeast Asia, where he had finally lost general Sodu, decapitated in battle while leading an expedition against the Chams in 1285. Apart from a couple of defensive actions in Burma, Temür took a different tack. He kept his soldiers and sailors out of southeast Asia, and he tried to make peace with the Japanese as well.[14]

The official Chinese history of the Yuan dynasty gives no account of Zhou's mission, and from that we may conclude that it was not an outstanding success—though the fact that the Cambodians later sent tribute to China may mean that it was not a complete failure, either. Nor have Chinese historians left any record of who led the mission, though in chapter 12 of his book Zhou does make a familiar-sounding mention of someone called Esen Khaya (Turkic for "Sound Rock"), suggesting he could conceivably have been the person concerned.

As to why Zhou was selected to join the mission, we can infer that he was from a well-connected trading or official family, perhaps one of the families the Mongols classified as a "scholar family (*ru hu*)."[15] He may also have been something of a linguist, and taken along to help as an interpreter. His book is peppered with Khmer and Sanskrit expressions, all picked up in just a year or so, in contrast to Marco Polo's memoirs, which scarcely mention any Chinese words despite the seventeen years he claims to have spent in China. Then again, Zhou is a competent chronicler, so perhaps he was charged with keeping some kind of written record. During the Song dynasty it had been the custom of envoys to keep quite detailed records of countries visited, and there is no reason to believe this practice was changed in Mongol times.

Whatever his role, the mission gave Zhou an opportunity to spend time in Cambodia looking and learning. Once in the Cambodian capital Yasodharapura, there seemed to be no rush to leave, and Zhou stayed on for nearly a year before returning home. While he was there he stayed with a family, either a Cambodian family or more likely the family of a local Chinese. Through them he learned about the Cambodian way of childbirth as well, we can assume, as many other aspects of life in Angkor. "Although I could not get to know the land, customs, and affairs of state of Cambodia in every particular," he writes in his preface, "I could see enough to get a general sense of them."

Zhou returned home in 1297, and we then lose track of him almost completely. A small clue to his later career comes from his *hao* or assumed name, which at least two Ming dynasty editions of his book provide. This assumed name, Thatched Courtyard Recluse (*Cao ting yimin*), may just have been a philosophical nod in the direction of Buddhist or Daoist seclusion. But given the fact that Zhou never achieved fame as a senior official, it may rather suggest that he was either unable to seek public office or too disaffected to do so. Disaffection was a common sentiment among Chinese scholars during the period of Mongol rule in China, when a strong sense of difference often divided cultivated Chinese from the Mongols, whom the Chinese regarded as uncouth and ill-mannered, not to mention foul-smelling. This sense of difference was reinforced by the Mongols' policy of classifying their subjects into people of different types, and by their suspension until 1315 of the imperial examination system, the customary Chinese ladder to high office. Some Chinese scholars were so disaffected that they refused to use Mongol reign-titles and other indications of Mongol status, but Zhou was clearly not one of these, since he refers respectfully to the Mongols and uses their reign title at the beginning of his narrative.[16]

The only other things we know about the older Zhou are that his book was completed within fifteen years of returning home—since it is referred to in another work published in or before 1312—and that he wrote the preface to a third work published in 1346. This tells us that he was still alive in that year, and from that we can deduce that he was a young man, probably still in his twenties, when he went to Cambodia in 1295. One other straw in the wind is the fact that there is a new word for "Siam" in Zhou's preface that only came into use some time after 1349–1350. Assuming he wrote or revised the preface himself, this suggests that he was still alive mid-century. Of his eventual death we know nothing.[17]

So much for Zhou's own life and times. But what of the country where he stayed in 1296–1297? Born as he was to believe in the supremacy of all things Chinese, Zhou must have been taken aback by the size and splendor of Angkor, still an extraordinary civilization at its height, or at least not yet obviously on the wane. What he saw and described was the outcome of nearly five centuries of political and cultural continuity, centered from the tenth century onward on the city of Yasodharapura. This culture of Angkor developed under a succession of kings who derived their authority from their "proximity to the sacred," to borrow the historian Michael Vickery's phrase.[18] This was usually a proximity to the Hindu deity Siva, who in Angkor carried overtones of ancestral spirits, though in the case of Suryavarman II, the twelfth-century king who built Angkor Wat, the deity was Vishnu.

Royal power was exercised at the apex of a social structure that depended on an elaborate system of slavery and varying degrees of servitude, and on the maintenance of a priesthood and temple foundations. The king oversaw the construction of temples, monuments, and artificial lakes, the disbursement of land, and the management of resources. The lakes or reservoirs may have been part of a centrally managed irrigation system to promote agricultural production, providing the essential source of royal authority, or may just have been symbols of royal sanctity and power.

In the century or so prior to Zhou's visit, Angkor was affected by a series of major changes. Historians still differ in their interpretation of what happened and how, but it seems that in the 1170s fighting between an expansionist Angkor and Cham forces culminated in the destruction of much of the Angkor capital. A warrior prince then reestablished Angkor's authority, and assumed the throne under the name of Jayavarman VII. He seems to have held sway less as a worshipper of Siva or Vishnu than as a Mahayana Buddhist. He applied his authority to overseeing a huge building program and bringing Buddhist belief into the heart of Angkor's life and iconography.

Jayavarman rebuilt Yasodharapura, putting up new city walls and causeways, massive tasks of construction and sculpture that Zhou Daguan describes in the first chapter of his book.[19] A new temple was the centerpiece of the new city. This was Bayon, which Zhou Daguan describes as having a gold tower, eight gold Buddhas, and a golden bridge flanked by gold lions leading to it. The huge stone faces staring out from Bayon with an air of serene complacency are sometimes said to be Jayavarman's own, while the unique reliefs at Bayon showing people eating, trading, traveling on ox-carts and in palanquins, and engaging in hand-to-hand fighting give us a rare look at the lives of the ordinary people of Angkor, and may embody in some way the compassionate view of the world Jayavarman derived from his Buddhism.

Within his new city walls Jayavarman retained structures built much earlier, including Bapuon, which Zhou describes as an "exquisite" bronze tower even taller than Bayon, and Phimeanakas, which Zhou tells us is where the king had a nightly tryst with a snake woman. An inscription from the end of Jayavarman's reign compares his relationship with his rebuilt city to that of a bridegroom and bride. "The town of Yasodharapura," it declares,

> decorated with powder and jewels, burning with desire, the daughter of a good family . . . was married by the king in the course of a festival that lacked nothing, under the spreading dais of his protection.

Jayavarman VII also built rest houses on roads linking the capital with other towns—which Zhou also remarks on—as well as hospitals and other temples, including the temple at Neak Pean in the Jayatataka reservoir, which Zhou calls the North Lake. Zhou describes Neak Pean as "a gold tower, square in shape, with several dozen stone chambers," though he does not mention its likely symbolic role as a representation of Lake Anavatapta. In Buddhist belief Anavatapta was the source of the four great rivers of the world, and of the power and authority of great Buddhist rulers from the time of the emperor Asoka onward. Like Jayavarman, Asoka was a conqueror—he united India in the third century BCE—who became deeply devoted to Buddhism after his bloody victories in war.

The urgency with which Jayavarman VII reconstructed the capital may have reflected his age—he was over sixty when he became king—and also a sense of insecurity and pending change. During his reign and in the century that followed, new forces were being brought to bear on Angkor. The Chams remained a threat. Mongol ascendancy was gradually affecting the political geography of east Asia. Sea-borne trade between China and southeast Asia was growing, a trend attested to by Zhou, drawing Cambodians toward rivers and sea ports and away from inland areas.

At the same time the influence of Angkor over areas to the north and northwest was diminishing. As a reflection of this, a series of battles or wars took place between the Cambodians and the Siamese in the late thirteenth century, with very destructive consequences. In his description of the Cambodian countryside, Zhou notes briefly but bleakly that "as a result of repeated wars with the Siamese the land has been completely laid to waste." Growing in tandem with this Siamese influence was the spreading influence of Theravada Buddhism, the "Doctrine of the Elders," the older, simpler form of Buddhism that now holds sway in Sri Lanka, Burma, Thailand, Laos, and Cambodia.

The growing popularity of Theravada Buddhism does not seem to have been immediately reflected in the palace at Angkor. Jayavarman VIII, the king who reigned in the late 1200s, just before Zhou's visit, was an iconoclast who undid much of what Jayavarman VII sought to put in place, restoring a cult of Siva and presiding over the defacement of Buddhist icons. And while the new king on the throne during

Zhou's visit, Indravarman III, may have reversed the tide again, and almost certainly subscribed to some form of Buddhist belief, we cannot be sure exactly what it was. That, at any rate, is what we can deduce from Zhou's book, which portrays a society in which the king wore a crown suggestive of tantric power, and in which Theravada Buddhist monks were widespread and influential but shared their authority with Saivite priests and Hindu pandits or wise men.

Whether this approach to Buddhism was also true of the reigns of later kings at Angkor is hard to know. The last Sanskrit inscription in Angkor was written some thirty years after Zhou's mission, and no more great building projects were undertaken in the fourteenth century, at least none that endured. Within 135 years of Zhou's visit, Yasodharapura was sacked by Siamese troops. The capital moved to the south of the country, and the Angkor era came more or less to an end.[20]

I have been referring more and more to Zhou's writings, and at this point I want to turn to the text of *A Record of Cambodia—The Land and Its People* and consider in more detail what it tells us about Angkor in 1296–1297 and how it is put together.

The book is divided into a general preface and forty sections, probably thanks to later editors. I have called these sections chapters. Some of them are so brief as to be no more than a few sentences long. They are not arranged in a particularly coherent sequence, and it is tempting to think that some of them, at any rate, have been rearranged, and are not in their original order. The last chapter, for example, could very well be part of chapter 2, since both of them describe the king's royal audiences, and even the window where he sat when the audiences took place. Again, chapter 18, on the landscape, actually describes the landscape in the estuary of the Mekong, and would fit well into the preface, which is also partly about sailing up the Mekong. Then again, there are two chapters on the indigenous mountain people, whom Zhou calls savages, which would clearly be better if they were presented in sequence rather than broken up as they are now. The same applies to two chapters on language and the writing system.

As it proceeds, the book tells us a great deal about buildings in and around Yasodharapura, the homes people lived in, their bathing habits, their means of transport, the food they ate and how they ate it, and the clothes they wore and how they were made. There is also information, some of it in special sections, some of it presented piecemeal, about slaves, women, the ruling elite, the king and the royal house, the military, justice, the extent and administration of the state, overseas Chinese, trade, religion, sexuality, health, and agriculture.[21]

A vital component of Angkor's civilization was its population of slaves. Zhou makes it clear that Angkor was a slave-based society, in the sense that the majority of people in Angkor were slaves. He writes that most families had a hundred or more slaves, while only the poorest had none. The slaves he describes were purchased, through whose mediation he does not say, from the indigenous people of the mountains. Slaves had no formal social status and were at the mercy of their masters and mistresses.

Apart from the slaves bought from the "savages," there were certainly other kinds of slavery and servitude in Angkor, as other historical sources make clear, but Zhou does not mention them. He only touches in passing on one other form of servitude—that of a young girl subjected to the initiation rite of *zhentan*, who became the property of the monk performing the rite if she was not redeemed by gifts. But there were clearly many other groups under forms of obligation and subservience, including the concubines in the royal palace, and indeed the whole population when called upon to wage war.

Zhou's account of the life of women is quite a full one. He notes that the local traders were all women. He portrays women, at least those from elite families, as confident, mobile, and ready to mix with other classes. The ceremonial offering of ripe rice to the Buddha in the seventh lunar month of the year was witnessed by a huge audience of women—and, it would seem, women only—riding in chariots and on elephants. "Without the slightest embarrassment" women from the great houses joined the thousands of women who regularly bathed in the river near the capital. Chinese sometimes came to watch them, and even join in—an irresistible temptation, perhaps, considering the fact that bathing was also a much-loved practice in south China, but bathing of a much more modest kind, in which a well-educated Chinese would not dream of bathing in the company of a woman.

As far as the women in the palace are concerned, Zhou describes their appearance but tells us nothing about how they led their lives, though he does portray the king's principal wife as a resourceful woman responsible for her husband's accession to the throne. The permanent female residents of the palace, including concubines and others, Zhou numbers at four to five thousand—which if true would have meant that the royal palace was crowded and densely populated. In addition he mentions a thousand or two servant women called *chenjialan*, as well as a female palace guard, probably the women responsible for carrying the king's palanquin. Among the priests there were women Saivites, though no Buddhist nuns.

Zhou's account of ordinary people's lives is otherwise quite sketchy. We learn little about children, other than the fact that young girls went through the *zhentan* initiation ceremony and that young boys served as Buddhist monks at school. Ordinary men get relatively little consideration, or at least explicit consideration, since Zhou rarely specifies that a person is male, using instead the gender-neutral terms *ren* (person) and *min* (people). In addition to serving as officials, pandits, priests, and monks, men are portrayed as working as carpenters and boat-builders, farmers and soldiers—though in all these cases Zhou writes about "people" rather than men as such, and the farming, at any rate, would have been women's work at least as much as it was men's.

Zhou's descriptions of the ruling elite are also sketchy. He tells us about its appurtenances—the carefully graded parasols, palanquins, and clothing material used by the different ranks of officials, and the large houses with partly tiled roofs where the king's relatives and high officials lived. The emphasis on clothes, parasols, and the like is not surprising—Zhou himself came from a culture in which there was an intense interest in the various forms of clothing, parasols, and so on, that were worn by officials of different ranks and reflected a person's status. Zhou also tells us about the monthly games and rituals that took place, evidently under elite patronage. But he does not give us a sense of the economic and administrative arrangements on which the power and authority of the elite were based. He makes no mention, for example, of institutions and practices that the inscriptions at Angkor describe, including temple foundations and the acquisition of wealth through land. Nor does he explain how the "great houses" and "homes of the wealthy" came to be what they were.

The king and his palace are described in detail. Zhou tells us that he saw the king, Indravarman III, both in royal audience inside the palace and on parade outside the palace grounds. According to Zhou, the king went outside his palace more frequently than his security-conscious predecessor, the Hindu iconoclast Jayavarman VIII. By Zhou's account the king was willing to do so because he felt protected by a sacred piece of iron embedded in his body, though we can assume there were other reasons too—his more tolerant attitude to Buddhism among them. Zhou portrays the king as being at the center of diplomatic life, military affairs, and justice. The king invited foreign envoys to join him during celebrations, and was evidently in command of the army, though there was also a commander-in-chief, a role the king himself had played when the previous king, his father-in-law, was still alive. (Zhou implies that whoever commanded the army did an indifferent job. He suggests that the soldiers were poorly led—he refers to a lack of strategy in war—and notes that they were inadequately armed. He also tells us that there was mass conscription when the Siamese went to war with Angkor.)

Zhou tells us, in effect, that the people of Angkor nurtured a sense of just rule, and that the king was its embodiment. The king was the point of reference for any dispute among the ordinary people, even on a small matter, and was responsible for handing down royal punishments for offences committed. These punishments consisted of fines or, for serious offences, being buried alive or having one's nose, fingers, or toes cut off. The latter appears to have been the harshest of these amputations, since according to Zhou criminals without toes were the only people forbidden access to the capital city.

In an interesting aside on the relatively limited role of the state, Zhou notes that such offences did not include certain categories of wrongdoing that were dealt with directly by those concerned. These included adultery, theft, and disputes between families. Disputes between families were resolved by means of a "judgment of heaven" that involved individuals from both families sitting in two of the stone towers east of the palace—the towers opposite the Elephant and Leper King Terraces—until one of them fell visibly sick. This "judgment" process was managed entirely by the two families concerned. (According to the *Treatise on the Various Foreigners*, a thirteenth-century Chinese guide to foreign customs that Zhou refers to in his preface, in nearby Champa the means of settling such disputes was less forgiving—the disputants had to go through a crocodile pool, and the one who was in the wrong would be eaten by the crocodiles.) Allegations of theft involved a trial by ordeal, comparable to the trial by ordeal of witches in medieval Europe. The suspected thief's hand was plunged into boiling oil. If it was scalded, the person was held to be guilty; if not, the person was innocent. Likewise, Zhou notes that the disposal of dead bodies left outside a person's house was also entirely the responsibility of the householder, rather than the state.

Zhou tells us something, but not a great deal, about the administration of the state. He describes how it was undertaken by a hierarchy of officials, including a chief minister, an army commander, and an astronomer, and notes that the state itself consisted of either some ten or some ninety "prefectures" or administrative units. The text has a crucial variant here which allows for this very large divergence in the number of possible units, and so the information about prefectures is not particularly useful. Zhou does, however, give us the names of ten of them, some of which can be identified, and from them we can see that thirteenth-century Angkor, though possibly less extensive than earlier, was still larger than present-day Cambodia, stretching from the south of present-day Laos into the west of present-day Thailand and the southeast of present-day Vietnam.

The walls of the capital, Yasodharapura, were built with sloping ramparts on the insides of the walls, and with gates that were guarded and shut at night. Prefecture capitals were walled with wooden stockades, though Zhou does not say who they were intended to defend against (presumably Chams or Siamese, at least). Nor does he say how extensive the state's control was outside the prefectural townships, other than mentioning the presence in larger villages of an official responsible for security.

When assessing these remarks, we can only guess at the amount of traveling that Zhou did outside the capital, apart from his first and last trips in and out of the country. In one—possibly corrupt—passage about people's physical appearance, he claims to know about people living "in the ordinary localities," a phrase which in Chinese could refer to towns or villages and therefore could suggest some travel. And in describing the temples and towers in villages, the wooden stockades around towns, and the devastation of the land after the wars with Siam, he seems to be drawing on first-hand experience. At any rate, on these matters he does not indicate that his knowledge was only second-hand, as he does in some other parts of the book. (As I mentioned earlier, he seems to be scrupulous about indicating whether he is reporting something first- or second-hand. Thus he tells us that he saw the king in royal audience at his golden window, but only "heard" that the king sat on a lion pelt during the audience—no doubt because the pelt was out of sight below the window frame.) Perhaps it is reasonable to think that since he was in the country for a year or so, he managed to visit at least some of the locations outside the capital.

The Chinese—whom Zhou calls *Tang ren*, people of the Tang dynasty, in line with common usage outside China—were of considerable interest, both to Zhou and to his Chinese readers. Zhou makes it clear that an increasing number of Chinese were living and trading in Cambodia, and he portrays them a little critically. According to Zhou they were sometimes ill-tuned to local customs, shamefully gave gifts and custom to male prostitutes, and were sometimes desperate enough to have sex with slaves. Chinese sailors often ran away from their ships and settled down in Cambodia, because life was so easy there. On the other hand Zhou shows some sympathy for Chinese in difficulty. Since there were more Chinese doing trade in Cambodia than there had been earlier, Chinese no longer earned the high respect they once enjoyed, and were sometimes cheated or mistreated. And they were laughed at when they used lavatory paper.

In matters of trade the Chinese could do well if they took in a Cambodian woman who could advise them. Chinese gold and silver were in demand, as well as a range of other Chinese goods (most of which I mentioned earlier). These included Chinese-made beds, which local people had recently started using for the first time. Finally, more Chinese were dying in Cambodia, leading to an increase in the number of cremations.

In addition to the growing numbers of Chinese merchants, Zhou notes that in recent years Siamese had come to live and trade in Cambodia, especially as tailors, a detail that reinforces the impression that trade was growing. Cloth and clothing were sometimes made domestically but might also be imported from as far away as the "Western Seas" (somewhere in India?). Zhou implies a high volume of trade, noting that business was conducted with cash, cloth, silver, or gold, depending on the size of the transaction. He also notes that beeswax was traded in large quantities—the cargo of beeswax Zhou mentions may have weighed over seventy tons, a heavy load even for the junks of Quanzhou.

Zhou is informative about religious life, which he interprets in a Chinese way. He tells us that every family in Angkor practiced Buddhism, and that the boys served as Buddhist monks at school. He also notes that there were plenty of Buddhist monks and Buddhist temples, and that the monks were called *zhugu*, a term similar to the one used to address Theravada Buddhist monks in Siam. He describes these simple, even ascetic Buddhists as worshipping simply, and being dressed very much as Buddhist monks are dressed in Cambodia and some other Buddhist countries today. He also notes that they had temples and pagodas in the villages, and that they were wealthier than the Saivites, whom he misleadingly calls Daoists.

From all this we can deduce that Angkor had a large number of Theravada Buddhist monks, who were influential at court and represented beliefs that most people subscribed to. Theravada Buddhism did not have a monopoly on faith, though. Importantly, Zhou notes that the king sometimes wore "a gold crown, like the crown worn by the Holder of the Diamond." The Holder of the Diamond, or *vajradhara*, is the Buddha in the tantric or esoteric school of Buddhism; assuming Zhou's comment is more than just a passing comparison, it suggests a tantric Buddhist element to the king's worldview. Zhou notes that there were also learned men or pandits and people—priests, most likely, though Zhou never says as much—that we can reasonably assume were worshippers of Siva (again, "Daoists"). The pandits and Saivites—who could take the role otherwise reserved for Buddhist monks in the *zhentan* initiation rite for girls—would have been members of religious groups with beliefs relating to Hinduism.

Taken together, these comments suggest that in 1296–1297 both the elite and the ordinary people accepted a range of Hindu and Buddhist doctrines, and that Theravada Buddhism had yet to sweep the board. I have used the term Hindu, but local beliefs were clearly described in Hindu terms but grounded in Cambodian practices and interwoven with beliefs concerning other numina, such as the stone lingams worshipped by the "Daoists" and the nine-headed snake spirit that the king was said to couple with every night.

Zhou's view of the sexual life of Cambodians is conveyed in some detail, albeit from a resolutely male point of view. Overall, he gives the impression of a relaxed sexual culture. By Zhou's account, there was no prohibition against adultery, though in what sounds like a fairly strong disincentive a husband whose wife took a lover could torture the lover. Women were "lascivious," by which Zhou seems to mean they enjoyed sex. Following the *zhentan* initiation rite, girls as young as seven were left to their own devices until they married. Likewise, people were often promiscuous before being married, without this being frowned on. Sexual relations between slaves and their owners—their masters, that is, as the mistresses are again not mentioned—are portrayed as being beyond the pale. Zhou makes one apparent reference to sex workers, describing groups of Cambodians who gathered in the marketplace and sold sexual services to Chinese men.

Zhou has little to say about health, and makes no mention at all of the royal hospitals built by earlier kings to provide health services to the people. His most positive observation is about the restorative use of a poultice of hot rice and salt after childbirth. Otherwise he comments that people were frequently ill with malaria, dysentery, and leprosy. He mentions the widely believed story that there was once a "leper king" of Cambodia, a story now associated with a twelfth-century statue on display in the national museum in Phnom Penh.

Zhou tells us that when a person died the body was put out in a remote spot as carrion. As for the kings, their remains were buried in towers. He does not say which towers were the tombs of which kings, though he does refer to Angkor Wat as the tomb of Lu Ban, a mythical Chinese figure whose name he may have confused with the name of Suryavarman II, the king who built it (see note 15 for details).

Agriculture is a subject of central importance, since it formed the bedrock of Angkor's wealth and authority. Zhou gives us valuable information, though he leaves many parts of the picture missing. As I mentioned earlier, he notes that crops could be harvested three or four times a year, though he attributes this to equable temperatures and six months of rain, and does not make it clear whether these harvests are all from the same piece of land. He says nothing about irrigation, though this would have been essential for multi-cropping, even allowing for the easy-growing variety of wet or floating rice that he mentions. Nor does he discuss fertilization, except to say that the Cambodians regarded the use of nightsoil, commonly used in China, as unclean. He reports that plowing was done without cows, who were only used for pulling carts. He notes that the waters of the Tonle Sap Lake rose so high during the wet season that families living close to the lake had to move into the hills. In addition he mentions the cultivation of vegetables, including pepper, and the cultivation and sale of forest products such as rosewood and lac. Finally, his description of the lower Mekong Delta—dark forests, thick carpets of millet, and huge herds of wild buffalo—gives a vivid impression of a countryside of bountiful, unused plenty.

These, then, are some of features of Zhou's richly descriptive work. There are of course caveats to be made about the book, and before concluding I should mention a couple of these. Firstly, there is the question of the author's prejudices and assumptions. As always, the mindset of the author matters a good deal. I have already sketched out the background to Zhou's upbringing and way of looking at the world, but it is worth emphasizing that his views as an educated Chinese figure quite strongly in his writings and what he chooses to describe. Scholars such as Michael Vickery warn us not to be too influenced by Chinese and Sanskrit sources when assessing conditions in the Cambodia of Angkor; such cautions heighten our consciousness of Zhou's Chineseness, and of the Chinese perspectives he brings to bear.

Zhou is an observant traveler, but his writings bear the hallmarks of a Chinese traveler abroad, with their condescension, sometimes prurient interest in erotica, and earnest efforts to tabulate, elucidate, and observe exotica in language that readers back home will understand and enjoy. These qualities are typical of other imperial travelers, including English adventurers of Victorian and Edwardian times, so to some extent the hallmarks are those of an imperial traveler rather than just a Chinese one. Nevertheless, we know enough of the Chinese style in such writings to recognize its characteristics in Zhou's book.

This brings me to another concern, which is the patchiness of the book, or anyway what we have of it, particularly the fact that some matters are dealt with quite thoroughly and others hardly at all. I have already mentioned this, for example, when considering Zhou's description of agriculture. As David Chandler has remarked, we must be grateful for what Zhou has given us, while conscious of the fact that he leaves a number of questions unanswered. For example, his account of the ruling elite is frustratingly brief. His account of slavery is partial. His descriptions of religious beliefs and practices are seen through the distorting lens of Chinese doctrines, while his accounts of agricultural practices, though revealing, leave unanswered vital questions about the control of the land, the management of rice surpluses, and the role of irrigation.

More prosaically, Zhou's book does not contain the name of a single Cambodian, king or commoner. Indeed, he only mentions five names in the entire book, none of them Cambodian—Sodu, Khubilai's general who lost his head; Lu Ban, the mythical Chinese figure who may have been confused with King Suryavarman II; Esen Khaya, or "Sound Rock," who may conceivably have been the man who led Zhou's mission; a fellow Chinese called Xue; and Zhu Maichen, a Chinese official whose wife once famously left him. Some of these omissions are the result of Zhou's approach to his subject matter. Other omissions may be the result of cuts or adjustments made by editors working on Zhou's text after his lifetime. These editorial changes may themselves have reinforced prejudices (and here I am speculating, since we have no concrete evidence to prove this), for example by leaving in passages describing the king, or sexual mores, or strange tales such as the stealing of gall, while cutting out less sensational material. Yet other omissions may be due to the disappearance or loss of parts of the text as Zhou originally wrote it.

Parts of the text show clear signs of having been cut or mutilated. Moreover, the text as we have it now is very short—too short for a book of this kind, even allowing for the terse, lapidary quality of literary Chinese prose. At eight thousand five hundred or so Chinese characters, Zhou's text is much shorter than other Chinese works of the same type. For example, the much-read account of the Chinese monk Xuanzang's journey to India, written during the Tang dynasty, is a much longer and fuller work.

One persuasive piece of evidence that the text is very much briefer than it was originally comes from the seventeenth-century Chinese bibliophile Qian Zeng. Qian came from roughly the same part of the country as Zhou, living as he did in the town of Changshu, not far from the mouth of the Yangzi River and some two hundred and fifty miles north of Wenzhou. A careful book collector, Qian wrote about two versions of Zhou's work that were evidently in his possession, one a copy of a Yuan dynasty edition, and the other a version included in a Ming dynasty anthology called *Sea of Stories Old and New (Gu jin shuo hai)*. Qian was very disparaging about the second version, which he described as "muddled and jumbled up, six or seven tenths of it missing, barely constituting a book at all."[22]

Nowadays, so far as is known, there are no Yuan dynasty versions of Zhou's book left in existence, and the text in *Sea of Stories Old and New* (or minor variations on it) has become the version we rely on. If Qian Zeng was right, the loss of all the Yuan versions is truly a great one, since *Sea of Stories Old and New* only gives us a third of what Zhou wrote, and must therefore be a pale shadow of the original.

The text in *Sea of Stories Old and New* seems to have gained currency during the Ming dynasty, and was reproduced—minus the text on one leaf, or two pages—in a second version of the popular anthology *Boundaries of Stories (Shuo fu)*, published early in the Qing dynasty. (The first version, done in the Ming dynasty, also included Zhou's book, but for a long time it was not available.) This text was probably also the basis for the text in another late Ming compilation, *Past Histories Old and New (Gu jin yi shi)*. Thereafter more or less the same text was reproduced in various other collections. When Paul Pelliot came to translate Zhou's book in 1902, it was the version in *Sea of Stories Old and New* that he used; and the version in *Lost Histories Old and New* was the core text used by the modern Chinese editor Xia Nai when he worked on the text in the 1970s.

Xia Nai's annotated edition, completed in 1980 and published in Beijing in 2000, is an enormously helpful work, drawing on variants from thirteen editions, including the ones I have just mentioned. I have used his edition as the basis for my own translation, and have only diverged from the text that he proposes in a very few instances.

For all its missing pieces, *A Record of Cambodia—The Land and Its People* still stands on its own as a remarkable description of day-to-day conditions in Angkor. It breathes new life into the buildings, temples, friezes, sculptures, steles, and inscriptions that are otherwise all that is left to us. After reading Zhou Daguan you cannot look at the stone towers opposite the Elephant Terrace without thinking of trials by heavenly judgment. When you look at the plain stone edifice and worn stone lions of the Bayon, you will be reminded that this was once a gold tower flanked by lions covered in gold. As you walk through the local markets, you will picture the women of Angkor selling their wares—many of these wares from China, just as they are now. When you stroll around Phimeanakas and the grounds of the royal palace, you can picture it milling with guards, retainers, and the women of the palace. And when you stand on Elephant Terrace you can imagine the crowd watching the king's New Year firework display, delighted by the thunderous noise of the firecrackers—much as the crowd delights in the annual fireworks display in front of the palace in Phnom Penh today.

ON THIS TRANSLATION

PUTTING A SEVEN-HUNDRED-YEAR-OLD book into readable English is not easy to do, especially when the book is written by a subject of one country now very remote from us, about another country about which we understand even less. The language of Zhou Daguan's book does not make the task any easier, since literary Chinese is well-known for its concision, leaving much more unspoken than its equivalent in English.

When translating from Chinese into English there is always a choice between sticking closely to the wording of the original, an approach which allows for more accuracy but can result in heavy, awkward language, and making the English more fluent and natural, even though it may be free with the original. I have leaned toward staying faithful to the original, while still trying to provide a version that is easy to read and not stilted, as literary Chinese in English so often is. My goal has been to provide a reliable text whose origins in the Chinese language are not too intrusive.

In a few instances I have been driven to embellishing the text, if that is the right phrase, when a sense is implied but not explicit, or when there is a lack of continuity, or when something seems very awkward or out of place. For example, Zhou persistently describes the Cambodians as *fan*, "foreign" (a term sometimes translated "barbarian," though it has fewer negative connotations than some of the other Chinese words used for barbarians), but after a while repeated use of the word "foreign" jars in English, so I have usually translated it as "local." Whenever I have stretched or altered the text in this way I make a note of it in the endnotes. On a couple of occasions I have offered a translation of Chinese words or phrases that are in serious doubt, and in these cases, too, I have described what I have done in the endnotes. It might have been easier to leave these doubtful words in Chinese, but there are enough foreign words in Zhou's book as it is, so I have done my best to keep to English whenever I can.

There are other, more specific problems to be dealt with when translating Zhou Daguan's text. Firstly there is the fragmentary condition of the text itself, which I mentioned in the introduction. It seems to be corrupt, or missing parts, or both. Parts of it may also have been rearranged. It is not so easy, though, to remedy these shortcomings. While you sometimes get a sense that the narrative is bumping along in a particularly disjointed way, it is usually not very clear where the missing, corrupted, or displaced passages are. In the end I have taken the easy way out and depended mostly on the text as defined by Xia Nai in his 2000 edition of the book. Xia's is as judicious a choice of text as we are likely to get, at least for now, and I have followed it with only a few exceptions. When I do make an exception I have, again, made a note of it in the endnotes.

Then there are the transliterations of Cambodian words which Zhou scatters through the book. Thanks to the pioneering work of the French scholars Paul Pelliot and George Coedès, as well as the invaluable work on the etymology of Khmer words done more recently by Michael Vickery and others, it is possible to have at least some sense of what these words may or may not be or mean. When that is so I have listed possible explanations in the endnotes. The process has, however, been a very rough and ready one. To tackle the task systematically we need to have a far better understanding of the Khmer and Chinese languages—their sound systems, etymologies, and so on—in the thirteenth century than we have now.

One particular problem in dealing with old Chinese transliterations of words in other languages like Khmer is that Chinese being a non-alphabetic writing system, its sound system has changed over time without us knowing exactly how. This being the case it is hard to know how Zhou Daguan would have pronounced the Chinese he wrote, even assuming he used a standard pronunciation of some kind. Fortunately we can benefit from the valuable efforts of several scholars to reconstruct the way Chinese was pronounced in earlier times. I have depended heavily on the 1991 lexicon of the sound of speech in the Yuan capital Dadu in 1300 CE drawn up by the linguist and historian Edwin G. Pulleyblank. Pulleyblank's work partially eclipses earlier, pioneering work on the sound of Chinese in the Tang capital Chang'an around 600 CE, done in the 1930s by the Swedish scholar Bernhard Karlgren. (China in the year 600 was, of course, almost as distant in time from the China of Zhou Daguan as we are today, so even without Pulleyblank's system Karlgren's sound reconstructions are only moderately useful.) Wherever Pulleyblank's or Karlgren's reconstructed sounds seem helpful I have given them in square brackets, with a P for Pulleyblank and a K for Karlgren.[23]

Pulleyblank's and Karlgren's systems involve the use of diacritical marks and special letters, most of which I have simplified. For example in Pulleyblank's lexicon what I have written as the letter 'h' should be given as a raised 'h,' indicating voiceless aspiration, while what I have written as 'e' encompasses various vowel sounds that Pulleyblank differentiates between. For those who want a less rough-and-ready rendering I have provided page references to both Pulleyblank's and Karlgren's lexicons whenever I cite them.

I have also simplified the Sanskrit transliterations, which I have based on R. S. McGregor's Hindi dictionary, with its helpful Sanskrit derivations. (I know a little Hindi but virtually no Sanskrit). For the transliteration of Khmer words I have used the simple, easy-to-read transliterations developed by David Smyth and Tran Kien for their *Practical Cambodian Dictionary*.

Translating the names of places and things in Zhou's book can be difficult. The names we now have for the buildings and other structures of Angkor—Bayon, Bapuon, and so on—are not the names they were known by when they were built. Nor are they the names Zhou uses for them. He calls them by simple names like "Stone Tower" and "North Lake" that describe what they are or where they are located. It is hard to know whether he does this because they are the names he was given for these places, or because he has simply decided for one reason or another to identify them by describing what they look like. Literary Chinese does not have the equivalent of capital letters or other markers for proper names, so the form of the text does not help us here. In the main text I have given the names for buildings and structures as Zhou gives them, with the names they are known by now in square brackets in cases where we can be fairly sure of a correct identification. I have translated them variously as proper names or simply as descriptive nouns as seems fit.

One particular issue is the name of the capital city. From the tenth to the fourteenth century it was called Yasodharapura, after Yasovarman I, the king who founded it. Today it is known as Angkor Thom. The latter is the name used for the city as defined by Jayavarman VIII, that is to say the area within the city walls that encloses Bayon, the Royal Palace, Elephant Terrace, and so on. Angkor Thom is not the same as Angkor. On its own the word Angkor tends to be used for the whole complex of structures in and around Angkor Thom, including structures outside the city walls such as Angkor Wat,

Bakheng, the lakes or barays, and other temples further afield. It is also used to refer to the state of which these structures were once a part. I have used the term Angkor in this latter way, to refer to the state whose thirteenth-century capital was Yasodharapura. I have used the names Yasodharapura or Angkor Thom to denote the capital city itself.

While on the subject of names, another issue concerns the names of all the trees, plants, herbs, animals, birds, fish, and other marine life that Zhou writes about. I am not a specialist in the flora and fauna of thirteenth-century Cambodia and China, and I have tried to identify the species Zhou refers to by drawing on both modern Chinese terminology and earlier Chinese usages, and also on what is known about Angkorian flora and fauna from other sources. (The work of the British scholar Judith Jacob, who has listed references to flora and fauna in Angkor inscriptions, is helpful here.) Clearly this is not an ideal approach, as the Chinese names of plants and animals have changed over time, and anyway they differ from region to region. An additional concern is that what Zhou describes in Chinese terminology may not be accurate in terms of Cambodian realities. I console myself with the thought that it is probably no use striving to be too exact. For one thing, Zhou himself may not always have known exactly what bird or herb he was describing, any more than he knew very precisely about, say, Cambodian religious doctrines.

Chinese names are given in the most common form of Chinese romanization, *pinyin*, with the surname first in the usual manner. For names in central Asian languages I have followed the practices of volume 6 of the *Cambridge History of China*.

With one exception I have given Chinese weights and measures in their non-metric English equivalents, with the original amounts and metric equivalents given in endnotes. The exception is li, the Chinese mile, roughly a third of an English mile or half a kilometer. I have left references to *li* as they are, since the word is now part of the English language—at any rate, it is listed in the standard English dictionaries.

For dates I have used the terms Common Era (CE) and Before the Common Era (BCE) rather than AD and BC. Dates in the text have been left in their Chinese form—"in the sixth month of the year *dingyou*" and so on—with the equivalent CE year given in brackets.

The notes at the end of the text give sources and more detailed information.

NOTES

Introduction

1. A more accurate and fuller translation into English of the title of the book by Zhou Daguan 周達觀, *Zhenla fengtu ji* 真臘風土記 would be "*A Record of the Customs of the People and the Geographical Characteristics of Cambodia.*" The edition of Zhou Daguan's work that I have used for this book is XN. The most accessible full edition of Marco Polo is H. Yule, ed., *The Travels of Marco Polo: The Complete Yule-Cordier Edition* (New York: Dover Publications, 1993). I have used R. Latham, *Marco Polo: The Travels* (London: Penguin Books, 1958). For the complex history of the many and varied versions of Marco Polo's memoirs, and the many differing views as to their veracity, see J. Larner, *Marco Polo and the Discovery of the World* (New Haven and London: Yale University Press, 1999). For a skeptical view of whether Marco Polo went to China, see F. Wood, *Did Marco Polo Go to China?* (Boulder: Westview Press, 1996), esp. 140–151.

2. I should note here that Zhou has been translated from Chinese into other languages, including Japanese and modern Chinese. There is also a translation of Zhou's work into Khmer, done from the Chinese in the 1960s by a group of scholars led by a Chinese Cambodian scholar, Lee Tiam-teng. The pirated version of the 1973 edition of his book is still for sale at Cambodian bookstalls.

3. The first substantial official Chinese account of Cambodia after Zhou's death is the section on Cambodia in *Ming shi* 明史, the official history of the Ming dynasty, a work begun over three hundred years after Zhou's time and not completed until 1735—*Ming shi* ([1735] Beijing: Zhonghua shuju, 1974), *juan* 卷 323, 8394–8396. The official histories preceding *Ming shi* were *Yuan shi* 元史, the history of the Mongol Yuan dynasty, compiled in 1369–70, and *Song shi* 宋史, the history of the Song dynasty, compiled in 1343–44. *Yuan shi* covered the period Zhou lived in and could have been expected to have a section on Cambodia. In fact it hardly deals with Cambodia at all, despite having sections on relations with various other east and southeast Asian states including Annam, Burma, and Siam. So far as I am aware there are only four or so references to Cambodia

in the whole book, one of them to a tributary mission from Cambodia to the Yuan court in 1295. See *Yuan shi* ([1370] Beijing and Shanghai: Zhonghua shuju, 1976), especially *juan* 208, 4607–4671; XN, 39. As for *Song shi*, it refers to the period before Zhou's visit but was compiled some 46 years after it, so might have drawn on Zhou's work. The entry on Cambodia in *Song shi* is however very brief and shows little sign of Zhou's influence. *Song shi* ([1344] Beijing and Shanghai: Zhonghua shuju, 1977), *juan* 489, 14086–14087. The supposition that the *Ming shi* historians used Zhou's text is just that, a supposition, though much of the last part of the *Ming shi* account of Cambodia resembles Zhou's text quite closely, even to the point of using the same words and phrases. Here is an extract (my translation), which parallels portions of chapters 12, 16, 13, and 5 of Zhou's text, in that order.

> When people die their bodies are put out in the open country and left to the crows and vultures to eat. If they are eaten up quickly, this is seen as a blessed reward. When they are in mourning they just shave off their hair, the women cutting off a section of hair above the forehead the size of a coin. They say this recompenses close relatives. Their writing is done by dyeing black the skin of muntjaks, deer, or other animals. They use a powder to draw small lines on it which stays fast forever. They treat the tenth month as the beginning of the year, and always add an intercalary month in the ninth month. The night is divided into four watches. They also have people who understand astronomy, and can calculate the time of partial eclipses of the sun and the moon. The learned men there are called *banjie*, the Buddhist monks are *zhugu*, and the Daoists are *basi*. . . . The Buddhist monks all eat fish and meat, and make offerings of them to the Buddha—they just do not drink wine. (*Ming shi, juan* 323, 8396).

The collection by Qianlong is *Si ku quan shu* 四庫全書 (*Complete Collection of Written Materials in Four Stacks*): XN, 6. The memoir by Pelliot's student is D. Sinor, "Remembering Paul Pelliot, 1878–1945," in H. Walravens, *Paul Pelliot (1878–1945): His Life and Works—A Bibliography* (Bloomington: Indiana University Research Institute for Inner Asian Studies, 2001), XXXIV. For the text of Paul Pelliot's translation, in a revised version published after his death, see PP, 9–35. The text of Michael Smithies' translation has been published as M.

Smithies, tr. and ed., *The Customs of Cambodia by Zhou Daguan (Chou Ta-kuan)* (Bangkok: The Siam Society, 2001), 15–102. As noted in the introduction, earlier English versions include the 1967 rendering of the Pelliot text by J. Gilman d'Arcy Paul.

4. On Zhou Daguan's other names, see xn, 2. Zhou Dake 周達可 is the name given in Wu Qiuyan 吾邱衍, *Zhu su shan fang ji* 竹素山房集, which refers to Zhou's book and was published sometime before Wu's death in 1312. Zhou Jianguan 周建觀 is the name given in the annotated book list by the seventeenth-century bibliophile Qian Zeng 錢曾 in *Du shu min qiu ji* 讀書敏求集.

5. Yasheng Huang, "Zhejiang's rural entrepreneurs are a model for China," *The Financial Times* (London and Singapore), October 2, 2006, 15.

6. On Zhu Xi and his critics, especially the utilitarian Chen Liang, and on the utilitarians in Wenzhou, see H. Tillman, *Confucian Discourse and Chu Hsi's Ascendancy* (Honolulu: University of Hawai'i Press, 1992), 161–186; also J. Gernet, *A History of Chinese Civilization* (Cambridge: Cambridge University Press, 1996), 346.

7. On *nan xi* 南戲, the southern drama, see Zhang P. and Luo Y., *Zhongguo wenxue shi* 中國文學史 (Shanghai: Fudan daxue chubanshe, 1996), 117–130; also W. Nienhauser, Jr., ed., *The Indiana Companion to Traditional Chinese Literature, Volume 1* (Bloomington and Indianapolis: Indiana University Press, 1986), 636–637; and C. Mackerras, *Chinese Drama: A Historical Survey* (Beijing: New World Press, 1990), 27–30.

8. All the coastal ports have names ending in *zhou* 州, the original meaning of which was an island or a stretch of land surrounded by water. Under the Mongols the term referred to a unit of local government, and it is also the second part of the name of various towns in Hainan 海南 and on the coast of south and southeast China. On the political history and trade of Wenzhou 溫州, see CH, 2541–2542.

9. Marco Polo on Hangzhou can be found in Latham, *Marco Polo: The Travels*, 213–231.

10. Wu Zimu 吳自牧, *Gruel Dream* (*Meng liang lu*, 夢梁錄), is in *Congshu jicheng* 叢書集成 (Shanghai, 1939), 3219–3221, partly translated with comments in E. Balazs, *Chinese Civilization and Bureaucracy* (New Haven and London: Yale University Press, 1964), 82–100. The extract quoted here is on page 96. Balazs' translation gives the impression that there were only men in the restaurant, but there may have been women there too.

11. Zhou mentions Sodu (Suodu, 唆都) in his preface. On Sodu's southern campaign, see M. Rossabi, "The reign of Khubilai khan," in CHC, 435. On the devastation of north China and its terrible loss of population, see F. Mote, "Chinese society under Mongol rule, 1215–1368," in CHC, 621.

12. Giovanni dei Marignolli and Ibn Battuta are cited in G. Hudson, *Europe and China* (London: Edward Arnold, 1931), 163.

13. On Quanzhou as a fleet harbor and shipyard, see CHC, 435, 482, 487; H. A. R. Gibb, tr. and ed., *Ibn Battuta: Travels in Asia and Africa, 1325–1354* (Delhi: LPP, 1999), 287–288. On junks and Yuan dynasty shipping, see J. Needham, *Science and Civilization in China, Volume 4, Physics and Physical Technology, Part III* (Cambridge: Cambridge University Press, 1971), 460–482, quoting Zhou Qufei 周去非's contemporary observation that the ships were "like houses," and identifying *chuan* 船 as likely to be the Chinese word for trading junk. Zhou Daguan mentions the beeswax cargo and the junk in chapter 19, and the gooseneck barnacles in chapter 26.

14. On Khubilai's military expeditions to Japan and southeast Asia, and the loss of Sodu, see Rossabi, "The reign of Khubilai khan," in CHC, 482–487; M. Rossabi, *Khubilai Khan: His Life and Times* (Berkeley, Los Angeles, and London: University of California Press, 1988), 206–228; M. Stuart-Fox, *A Short History of China and Southeast Asia: Tribute, Trade and Influence* (Crows Nest, New South Wales: Allen and Unwin, 2003), 59–72; and G. Coedès, *The Indianized States of Southeast Asia* (Honolulu: University of Hawaii Press, 1996), 192. On Temür's foreign policy, see Hsiao Ch'i-ch'ing, "Mid-Yüan politics," in CHC, 501–504.

15. The Mongols' system of classifying their subjects is described in Tao Zongyi 陶宗儀, *Chuo geng lu* 輟耕錄 (*Interrupted Labors*). There were four main classifications: Mongols, various non-Chinese races, Chinese and Sinified people

of north China, and the "new subjects" of southern China. *Ru hu* 儒戶, "scholar family," was a sub-category. Tao's work is summarized in Gernet, *A History of Chinese Civilization*, 368–369; see also Mote, "Chinese society under Mongol rule," in CHC, 629–632. Incidentally Tao was from the town of Taizhou 台州, so he and Zhou were near-neighbors. Tao included Zhou's work in his popular anthology *Shuo fu* 說郛 (*Boundaries of Stories*) a Ming copy of which was republished in 1927. The text of this 1927 edition, which contains useful textual variants, is referred to later here as the "Ming *Shuo fu*" text: XN, 6, 191.

16. On disaffection among Chinese scholars during the Mongol era, see F. Mote, "Confucian Eremitism in the Yuan Period," in Arthur Wright, ed., *The Confucian Persuasion* (Stanford: Stanford University Press, 1960), 202–240.

17. The book published in 1312 that referred to Zhou's work was Wu Qiuyan 吾邱衍, *Zhu su shan fang ji* 竹素山房集. The work published in 1346 was Lin Kun 林坤, *Cheng zhai za ji* 誠齋雜記 (*Cheng Zhai's Miscellany*)—details are in XN, 2. (The latter may contain a lost sentence from Zhou's book, as discussed in note 9.)

It is perfectly possible that Zhou lived till the 1350s. It was not unusual for people of the time to live into their eighties. Tao Zongyi, for example, editor of *Boundaries of Stories*, was born in 1316 and lived until he was 87.

18. M. Vickery, *Society, Economics and Politics in Pre-Angkor Cambodia: The 7th–8th Centuries* (Tokyo: Toyo Bunko, 1998), 408.

19. Or at least he started to rebuild it. New scholarship by Claude Jacques proposes a new interpretation of an old inscription that would mean that Jayavarman VII's successor Indravarman II reigned for 50 rather than 23 years, allowing for almost 90 years of Buddhist rule before the Buddhist iconoclast Jayavarman VIII acceded to the throne. See http://conferences.arts.usyd.edu.au/viewabstractphp?id=619&cf=9.

20. "More or less" since Angkor Wat continued to be used in one form or another, while the transfer of the capital south may have reflected a change of priorities rather than the waning of a civilization. The fact remains though that by the 1430s the characteristic qualities and geographical focus of Angkor were at an end.

For an overview of the last few centuries of Angkor, see D. Chandler, *A History of Cambodia* (Boulder and Oxford: Westview Press, 2000), 55–76; also 47–48 on slaves, and 66 for the inscription about Jayavarman VII's marriage to Yasodharapura. Further insights can be found in C. Higham, *The Civilization of Angkor* (Berkeley and Los Angeles: University of California Press, 2001), 107–166; C. Jacques, *Angkor* (Köln: Könemann, 1999); L. Briggs, *The Ancient Khmer Empire* (Philadelphia: American Philosophical Society, 1951), 223–252; and B. Groslier, *Indochina* (London: Barrie and Jenkins, 1970), 93–115.

21. Zhou's comments on Angkor include the following:

(a) The family he stayed with: chapter 7.

(b) Slaves: chapters 8 (*zhentan*), 9 (slaves from indigenous people), 11 (indigenous people), 39 (mass conscription).

(c) Women: chapters 5 (women priests), 6 (concubines, *chenjialan*), 7 (when husbands away), 8 (*post-zhentan*), 13 (*harvest festival*), 20 (markets), 37 (bathing), 40 (kings' wife, palace guard)—Zhou's discussion of bathing in Cambodia may be compared with the discussion of bathing in South China in J. Gernet, *Daily Life in China on the Eve of the Mongol Invasion 1250–1276* (London: George Allen & Unwin, 1962), 123–125.

(d) Men, children, and families: chapters 2 (homes), 4 (men as officials), 5 (boys at school, men as priests and monks), 8 (girls post-*zhentan*), 17 (men—and women—as farmers), 30 (home utensils and furniture), 32 (men as carpenters and boatbuilders), 39 (men as soldiers).

(e) The ruling elite: chapters 2 (residences), 3 (dress), 4 (parasols and palanquins), 2, 8, 13, and 30 ("great houses," *fudi* 府第 and "wealthy homes," *fu shi* 富室, *fu jia* 富家)—Compare the discussion of clothes and parasols in China in Gernet, *Daily Life in China on the Eve of the Mongol Invasion*, 128–129.

(f) The king and palace: chapters 2 (building, royal audience), 3 (dress), 6 (wives, concubines, *chenjialan*, royal audience), 13 (New Year's fireworks, seventh-month dances), 14 (royal justice), 16 (burial), 40 (parade, audience).

(g) Disputes and justice: chapters 1 (amputees excluded from the city), 14 (disputes and justice, disposing of the dead).

(h) The administration of the state: chapters 1 (capital city walls), 4 (official hierarchy), 33 (prefectures, stockades), 34 (village officials).

(i) Overseas Chinese: chapters 3 (unsuitable dress), 6 (male sex workers), 9 (sex with slaves), 20 (getting local women's advice, diminishing respect to traders as their numbers increase), 37 (women bathing), 38 (sailors running away).

(j) Trade: chapters 3 (trade in cloth), 11 (savages cultivating cardamom, kapok), 19 (ivory, rhinoceros horn, beeswax, kingfisher feathers), 20 (using gold, silver, cloth), 21 (sought-after Chinese items), 29 (Siamese silk workers and tailors).

(k) Religion: chapters 2 (snake spirit), 3 (king's crown), 5 (pandits, Buddhist monks, Saivites, lingams, places and styles of worship, boys at school), 8 (monks, priests, and *zhentan*), 34 (Buddhist temples and towers in villages).

(l) Sexuality: chapters 6 (sex workers), 7 ("lascivious" women and husbands away), 8 (*zhentan*, promiscuous young men), 9 (sex with slaves), 14 (adultery, torture of wife's lover), 15 (bathing and leprosy), 37 (bathing), 38 (Chinese obtaining women easily).

(m) Health: chapters 7 (childbirth and poultices), 14, 16 (disposal of dead bodies), 15 (washing, leprosy, dysentery, medicines, witchdoctors).

(n) Agriculture: chapters 17 (multicropping, plowing, flooding around Tonle Sap Lake, nightsoil), 18 (lower Mekong landscape), 19 (forest products, peppers), 24 (cows and carts), 25 (vegetables).

22. Qian Zeng's comments are reproduced as part of appendix 2 of XN, 189. A full account of the textual history of Zhou's book, including the versions in *Gu jin shuo hai* 古今海, the two very different editions of *Shuo fu* (*Boundaries of Stories*) 說郛, and *Gu jin yi shi* (*Lost Histories Old and New*) 古今逸史 appear in XN, 191–203, with a summary of the texts he cites on 6–9. Also see the earlier, supplementary material in PP, 37–55.

On this translation

23. Pulleyblank's and Karlgren's systems of writing the sounds of old Chinese vary markedly from the *pinyin* or romanization system most often used now to transliterate Chinese. This sometimes has the effect of making their renderings of sounds look more remote from present-day pronunciation than they are. Pulleyblank's lexicon is in E. Pulleyblank, *Lexicon of Reconstructed Pronunciation in Early Middle Chinese, Late Middle Chinese, and Early Mandarin* (Vancouver: UBC Press, 1991), referred to from now on as LRP. For Karlgren see B. Karlgren, *Grammata Serica Recensa* (Stockholm: Museum of Far Eastern Antiquities, 1964), referred to from now on as GSR.

A RECORD OF CAMBODIA
THE LAND AND ITS PEOPLE

GENERAL PREFACE

THE COUNTRY OF Zhenla, also called Zhanla, calls itself Ganbozhi [Cambodia]. The present sacred dynasty follows the Buddhist scriptures of the Tibetans and gives it the name of Ganpuzhi, which sounds almost the same as Ganbozhi.[1]

If you set sail from Wenzhou and go south-southwest by the compass past Min, Guang, and the various overseas ports, then cross the Seven Islands Sea and the Jiaozhi Sea, you come to Champa; and with the wind behind you, you will then get from Champa to Zhenpu on the frontier of Cambodia in about fifteen days.[2]

From Zhenpu you carry on west-southwest by the compass, cross the Kunlun Sea, and enter a river estuary. There are dozens of estuaries but you can only go into the fourth one, as the rest are all so silted up that very large boats cannot get through. As it is, there are tall bamboos, old trees, yellow sand, and white reeds as far as the eye can see. As you move swiftly along it is not easy to make out where you are, and the sailors reckon it is a hard thing to find the right estuary.[3]

From the mouth of the estuary you sail north, and with a favorable current you reach a place called Zhanan, a prefecture of Cambodia, in about fifteen days. For the trip from Zhanan you change on to a small boat. With a favorable current it takes ten days or so to go past Halfway Village and Buddha Village, cross the Freshwater Sea [Tonle

Sap Lake], and reach a place called Ganpang, fifty *li* [roughly 17 miles or 25 kilometers] from the capital city.[4]

According to the *Treatise on the Various Foreigners*, Cambodia is seven thousand *li* in breadth. Going north from the capital, it is fifteen days by road to Champa, and to the southwest it is fifteen days' journey to Siam. In the south it is ten days' journey to Fanyu, and to the east there is the ocean.[5]

It has long been a trading country.

The great Mandate of Heaven that the sacred dynasty has received includes everywhere within the four seas. Marshal Sodu set up a province in Champa, and sent out a general and a senior commander, who went there together. In the end they were seized and did not return.[6] In the sixth month of the year *youwei* in the Yuanzhen reign period (1295), the sacred Son of Heaven dispatched an envoy with an imperial edict, and ordered me to accompany him.[7]

In the second month of the following year, the year *bingshen* in the Yuanzhen reign period (1296), we left Mingzhou, and on the twentieth day of that month we set sail from the harbor at Wenzhou. On the fifteenth day of the third month we reached Champa, having been set back by adverse winds mid-journey. We arrived in Cambodia in the autumn, at the beginning of the seventh month.

We duly secured the submission of local officials. In the sixth month of the year *dingyou* in the Dade reign period (1297) we turned our boat around, and by the twelfth day of the eighth month we were back at Mingzhou, anchored off the coast.

Although I could not get to know the land, customs, and affairs of state of Cambodia in every particular, I could see enough to get a general sense of them.[8]

~: :~

1
THE CITY AND ITS WALLS

The walls of the city [Angkor Thom] are about twenty *li* [about 7 miles or 10 kilometers] in circumference. There are five gateways, each of them with two gates, one in front of the other. There are two gateways facing east, and one gateway facing in each of the other directions.[9] Around the outside of the city walls there is a very large moat. This is spanned by big bridges carrying large roads into the city. On either side of every bridge there are fifty-four stone deities. They look like stone generals, huge and fierce-looking.

The five gateways are all alike. The parapets of the bridges are all made of stone and carved into the shape of snakes, each snake with nine heads. The fifty-four deities are all pulling at the snake with their hands, and look as if they are preventing it from escaping. Above the gateways in the city wall there are five stone Buddha heads. Four of them face toward the four cardinal points, and one of them is placed in the middle. It is decorated with gold. On either side of the gates the stones are carved into the shape of elephants.[10]

The walls are all made of piled-up stones, and are about twenty-one feet high. The stones are very tightly packed and firm, so there are no weeds growing. There are no battlements either. Here and there sugar palms have been planted on the walls, and there are empty chambers at frequent intervals.[11]

The inside of the walls is built like a slope, and is probably over a hundred feet in width. The slopes all have big gates on them that shut at night and open early in the day. There are guards, too, though only dogs are not allowed in—and also criminals who have had their toes amputated.

The city walls form an exact square, with a stone tower on each of its four sides.

In the center of the capital is a gold tower [Bayon], flanked by twenty or so stone towers and a hundred or so stone chambers. To the east of it is a golden bridge flanked by two gold lions, one on the left and one on the right. Eight gold Buddhas are laid out in a row at the lowest level of stone chambers.[12]

About a *li* north of the gold tower there is a bronze tower [Bapuon]. It is even taller than the gold tower, and an exquisite sight. At the foot there are, again, several dozen stone chambers.[13]

About one *li* further north again there is the residence of the king [Royal Palace]. There is another gold tower [Phimeanakas] in his sleeping quarters.[14]

I suppose all this explains why from the start there have been merchant seamen who speak glowingly about "rich, noble Cambodia."

Half a *li* or so beyond the south gate is Stone Tower Mountain [Phnom Bakheng]. According to legend Lu Ban built it in a single night. Lu Ban's tomb [Angkor Wat] is about one *li* beyond the south gate. It is about ten *li* [five kilometers] in circumference, and has several hundred stone chambers.[15]

Ten *li* east of the city wall lies the East Lake [East Baray]. It is about a hundred *li* in circumference. In the middle of it there is a stone tower with stone chambers. In the middle of the tower is a bronze reclining Buddha with water constantly flowing from its navel.[16]

Five *li* to the north of the city wall lies the North Lake [Jayatataka Baray]. In the middle of it is a gold tower, square in shape, with several dozen stone chambers [Neak Pean]. A gold lion, a gold Buddha, a bronze elephant, a bronze cow, and a bronze horse—these are all there.[17]

∵ ∴

2

RESIDENCES

The royal palace, officials' residences, and great houses all face east. The palace lies to the north of the gold tower with the gold bridge [Bayon], near the northern gateway. It is about five or six *li* in circumference.[18] The tiles of the main building are made of lead; all the other tiles are made of yellow clay. The beams and pillars are huge, and are all carved and painted with images of the Buddha. The rooms are really quite grand-looking, and the long corridors and complicated walkways, the soaring structures that rise and fall, all give a considerable sense of size.

In the place for doing official business there is a gold window, with rectangular pillars to the left and right of the crosspieces. About forty or fifty mirrors are arrayed on either side of the upper part of the window; the lower part is made of images of elephants. I have heard that there are many wonderful places in the inner palace, but it is very strictly out of bounds and I could not get to see them.

Inside the palace there is a gold tower, at the summit of which the king sleeps at night. The local people all say that in the tower lives a nine-headed snake spirit which is lord of the earth for the entire country. Every night it appears in the form of a woman, and the king first shares his bed with her and has sex with her. Even his wives do not dare go in. At the end of the second watch he comes out, and only then can he sleep with his wives and concubines. If for a single night this spirit does not appear, the time has come for this foreign king to die. If for a single night he stays away, he is bound to suffer a disaster.[19]

Next come the dwellings of the king's relatives, senior officials, and so on. These are large and spacious in style, very different from ordinary people's homes. The roofs are made entirely of thatch, except for the family shrine and the main bedroom, both of which can be tiled. In every house the rooms are also made to a regulation size, according to the rank of the official living there.

At the lowest level come the homes of the common people. They only use thatch for their roofs, and dare not put up a single tile. Although the sizes of their homes vary according to how wealthy they are, in the end they do not dare emulate the styles of the great houses.

~: :~

3
DRESS

From the king down, the men and women all wear their hair wound up in a knot, and go naked to the waist, wrapped only in a cloth. When they are out and about they wind a larger piece of cloth over the small one.

There are very many different grades of cloth. The materials the king wears include some that are extremely elegant and beautiful, and worth three or four ounces of gold a piece. Although cloth is woven domestically, it also comes from Siam and Champa. Cloth from the Western Seas is often regarded as the best because it is so well-made and refined.[20]

Only the king can wear material with a full pattern of flowers on it. On his head he wears a gold crown, like the crown worn by the Holder of the Diamond.[21] Sometimes he goes without a crown, and simply wears a chain of fragrant flowers such as jasmine wound round the braids of his hair. Around his neck he wears a large pearl weighing about four pounds. On his wrists and ankles and all his fingers and toes he wears gold bracelets and rings, all of them inlaid with cat's-eye gemstones. He goes barefoot, and the soles of his feet and the palms of his hands are dyed crimson with a red preparation. When he goes out he has a gold sword in his hand.

Among ordinary people only the women can dye the soles of their feet and the palms of their hands. The men do not dare to.

Senior officials and relatives of the king can wear cloth with a scattered floral design, while junior officials and no others can wear cloth with a two-flower design. Among the ordinary people, only women can wear cloth with this design. However if a newly arrived Chinese wears it, people do not make so bold as to take offense, on the grounds that he is "*anding basha*," meaning that he does not understand what is right and proper.[22]

~: :~

4
OFFICIALS

As in China, the country has officials with the rank of chief minister, commander-in-chief of the army, astronomer, and so on. Below them are various kinds of junior officials, but they are not called by the same titles as ours. In general, those who take on these positions are the king's relatives. If they are not, they give him a daughter as a concubine as well.[23]

In going out and about, the insignia and retinues of these officials vary by rank. The most senior are those with a palanquin with gold poles and four parasols with gold handles.[24] Next in rank are those that have a palanquin with gold poles and two gold-handled parasols. Next down are those with a palanquin with gold poles and one gold-handled parasol; and next again, those with just one gold-handled parasol. At the lowest level are those who just have a parasol with a silver handle and nothing else. There are also those who have a palanquin with silver poles.

The senior officials with gold-handled parasols are all called *bading* or *anding*. Those with silver-handled parasols are called *siladi*.[25] The parasols are all made of a strong, thin red Chinese silk, with fringes that hang down and trail on the ground—except for oiled parasols, which are made of the same silk, but are green and have short fringes.

~: :~

5

THE THREE DOCTRINES

Those who are learned men are called *banjie*. Those who are Buddhist monks are called *zhugu*. Followers of the Dao are called *basiwei*.[26]

With regard to *banjie*, I don't know what the source of their doctrine is. They have nowhere that can be called an academy or place of learning, and it is hard to find out what books they study. All I have seen is that they dress like other people, except that they hang a white thread around their neck. This is all that distinguishes them as learned men. Those among the *banjie* who take up official positions become men of high status. They keep the thread round their neck till the end of their life.

Zhugu shave their heads and dress in yellow. They leave their right shoulder uncovered, and otherwise wrap themselves in a robe made of yellow cloth and go barefoot. For their temples they too can use tiles for roofing. In the middle of the temple there is just one icon, an exact likeness of the Sakyamuni Buddha, which they call *bolai*.[27] It is clothed in red, sculpted from clay, and painted in many colors. Apart from that there are no other icons. In the pagodas, the Buddhas are all different in appearance and all cast in bronze. There are no bells, drums, clappers, or cymbals, and no hanging curtains, fine canopies, and the like.

The monks all eat fish and meat—they just don't drink wine. They also make offerings of fish and meat to the Buddha. They take one meal a day, which they get from the home of an almsgiver, as there are no kitchens in the temples. They chant a very large number of scriptures, which are all written on piles of palmyra leaves put together in an extremely orderly way.[28] They write on them with a black script, using not brush and ink to write with but something else, though I don't know what. The monks also have palanquins and parasols with gold and silver poles and handles. If the king is dealing with important matters of government, he also seeks their advice. There are no nuns though.[29]

The *basiwei* dress just like ordinary people, except that they wear a red or white cloth on their head. It looks like the tall headdress of Tartar women, except it is somewhat shorter.[30] They have temples, too, though these are rather smaller than the Buddhist temples. In general the Daoists are less prevalent than the Buddhists. They don't make offerings to an icon, only to a block of stone, like the altar stones for the gods of the earth in China.[31] Again, I do not know what the source of their beliefs is. They do have women priests, though. Their temples can be roofed with tiles too. *Basiwei* don't eat other people's food, and don't let other people see them eat. Again, they don't drink wine. I have never seen them chanting scriptures or engaging in devotional studies.

When young boys from lay families go to school, they all start by being trained by Buddhist monks. Only when they have grown up do they return to lay life. I couldn't look into this in detail.

~: :~

6

THE PEOPLE

The one thing people know about southern barbarians is that they are coarse, ugly, and very black. I know nothing at all about those living on islands in the sea or in remote villages, but this is certainly true of those in the ordinary localities. When it comes to the women of the palace and women from the *nanpeng*—that is, the great houses—there are many who are as white as jade, but that is because they do not see the light of the sun.

Generally, men and women alike wrap a cloth around their waist, but apart from that they leave their smooth chests and breasts uncovered. They wear their hair in a topknot and go barefoot. This is the case even with the wives of the king.[32]

The king has five wives, one principal wife and one for each of the four cardinal points. Below them, I have heard, there are four or five thousand concubines and other women of the palace. They also divide themselves up by rank. They only go out of the palace on rare occasions.[33]

Every time I went inside the palace to see the king, he always came out with his principal wife, and sat at the gold window in the main room. The palace women lined up by rank in two galleries below the window. They moved to and fro to steal looks at us, and I got a very full view of them. Any family with a female beauty is bound to have her summoned into the palace.

At the lower level there are also the so-called *chenjialan*, servant women who come and go providing services inside the palace and number at least a thousand or two. In their case they all have husbands and live mixed in among ordinary people. They shave back the hair on the top of their head, which gives them the look of northerners with their "open canal" partings. They paint the area with vermilion, which they also paint on to either side of their temples. In this way they mark themselves out as being *chenjialan*. They are the only women who can go into the palace; no one else below them gets to go in. There is a continuous stream of them on the roads in front of and behind the inner palace.[34]

Apart from wearing their hair in a topknot, ordinary women do not have ornaments in their hair like pins or combs. They just wear gold bracelets on their arms and gold rings on their fingers. The *chenjialan* and the women in the palace all wear them too. Men and women usually perfume themselves with scents made up of a mixture of sandalwood, musk, and other fragrances.

Every family practices Buddhism.

There are a lot of effeminate men in the country who go round the markets every day in groups of a dozen or so.[35] They frequently solicit the attentions of Chinese in return for generous gifts. It is shameful and wicked.

∻ ∽

7
CHILDBIRTH

As soon as they give birth the local women prepare some hot rice, mix it with salt, and put it into the entrance of the vagina. They usually take it out after a day and a night. Because of this, women do not fall sick when they are giving birth, and usually contract so as to be like young girls again.[36]

When I first heard this I was surprised by it, and seriously doubted whether it was true. Then a girl in the family I was staying with gave birth to a child, and I got a full picture of what happened to her. The day after the birth, she took up the baby right away and went to bathe in the river with it. It was a truly amazing thing to see.

Then again, I have often heard people say that the local women are very lascivious, so that a day or two after giving birth they are immediately coupling with their husbands. If a husband doesn't meet his wife's wishes he will be abandoned right away, as Zhu Maichen was.[37] If the husband happens to have work to do far away, if it is only for a few nights that is all right, but if it is for more than ten nights or so the wife will say, "I'm not a ghost—why am I sleeping alone?" This is how strong their sexual feelings are. That said, I have heard that there are some who exercise self-restraint.

The women age very quickly indeed, the reason being that they marry and have children young. A twenty- or thirty-year-old woman is like a Chinese woman of forty or fifty.

~: ~

8
YOUNG GIRLS

When a family is bringing up a daughter, her father and mother are sure to wish her well by saying, "May you have what really matters—in future may you marry thousands and thousands of husbands!"

When they are seven to nine years old—if they are girls from wealthy homes—or only when they are eleven—if they come from the poorest families—girls have to get a Buddhist monk or a Daoist to take away their virginity, in what is called *zhentan*.

So every year, in the fourth month of the Chinese calendar, the authorities select a day and announce it countrywide. The families whose daughters should be ready for *zhentan* let the authorities know in advance. The authorities first give them a huge candle. They make a mark on it, and arrange for it to be lit at dusk on the day in question. When the mark is reached the time for *zhentan* has come.[38]

A month, fifteen days, or ten days beforehand, the parents have to choose a Buddhist monk or a Daoist. This depends on where the Buddhist and Daoist temples are. The temples often also have their own clients. Officials' families and wealthy homes all get the good, saintly Buddhist monks in advance, while the poor do not have the leisure to choose.

Wealthy and noble families give the monks wine, rice, silk and other cloth, betel nuts, silverware, and the like, goods weighing as much as a hundred piculs and worth two or three hundred ounces of Chinese silver. The smallest amount a family gives weighs ten to forty piculs, depending on how thrifty the family is.[39]

The reason poor families only start dealing with the matter when their girls reach eleven is simply that it is hard for them to manage these things. Some wealthy families do also give money for poor girls' *zhentan*, which they call doing good work. Moreover in any one year a monk can only take charge of one girl, and once he has agreed to and accepted the benefits, he cannot make another commitment.

On the night in question a big banquet with drums and music is laid on for relatives and neighbors. A tall canopy is put up outside the entrance to the house, and various clay figurines of people and animals are laid out on top of it. There can be ten or more of these, or just three or four—or none at all in the case of poor families. They all have to do with events long ago, and they usually stay up for seven days before people start taking them down.

At dusk the monk is met with palanquin, parasol, drums, and music and brought back to the house. Two pavilions are put up, made of colorful silk. The girl sits inside one, and the monk inside the other. You can't understand what he's saying because the drums and music are making so much noise—on that night the night curfew is lifted. I have heard that when the time comes the monk goes into a room with the girl and takes away her virginity with his hand, which he then puts into some wine. Some say the parents, relatives and neighbors mark their foreheads with it, others say they all taste it. Some say the monk and the girl have sex together, others say they don't. They don't let Chinese see this, though, so I don't really know.

Toward dawn the monk is seen off again with palanquin, parasol, drums, and music. Afterward silk, cloth, and the like have to be given to the monk to redeem the body of the girl. If this is not done the girl will be the property of the monk for her whole life and won't be able to marry anyone else.

The instance of this that I saw took place early on the sixth night of the fourth month of the year *dingyou* in the Dade reign period (1297).[40]

Before this happens, the parents always sleep together with their daughter; afterward, she is excluded from the room and goes wherever she wants without restraint or precaution. When it comes to marriage, there is a ceremony with the giving of gifts, but it is just a simple, easygoing affair. There are many who get married only after leading a dissolute life, something local custom regards as neither shameful nor odd.

On a *zhentan* night up to ten or more families from a single alley may be involved. On the city streets people are out meeting Buddhist monks and Daoists, going this way and that, and the sounds of drums and music are everywhere.

~: :~

9

SLAVES

Family slaves are all savages purchased to work as servants. Most families have a hundred or more of them; a few have ten or twenty; only the very poorest have none at all. The savages are people from the mountains. They have their own way of categorizing themselves, but are commonly called "thieving Zhuang."[41] When they come to the city, none of them dares go in and out of people's homes. They are so despised that if there is a quarrel between two city dwellers, it only takes one of them to be called a Zhuang for hatred to enter into the marrow of his bones.

A strong young slave is worth perhaps a hundred pieces of cloth; a weak old one can only fetch thirty or forty. They are only allowed to sit and sleep under the house.[42] If they are carrying out their tasks then they can come up into the house, but they must kneel, join their hands in greeting, and bow down to the floor before they can venture forward. They address their master as *batuo* and their mistress as *mi*. *Batuo* is "father," and *mi* is "mother."[43] If they do something wrong they are beaten, and take their caning with heads bowed, not venturing to move even a little.

The males and females mate together, but the master would never have reason to have intercourse with them. Sometimes a Chinese who comes to Cambodia and has long been single will act carelessly, but as soon as he has had relations with one of them the master will hear of it, and the following day he will refuse to sit with the Chinese, on the grounds that he has come into contact with a savage.

Sometimes one of them will have intercourse with an outsider, to the point of becoming pregnant and having a baby. But the master won't try and find out where it is from, since the mother has no status and he will profit from the child, who can eventually become his slave.

Sometimes slaves run away. Those that are caught and taken back must carry a dark blue tattoo on their face, and sometimes an iron shackle around their neck or between their arms and legs.[44]

～ ～

10
LANGUAGE

The country's language consists of sounds that are its own, and despite being nearby, neither the Chams nor the Siamese can make themselves understood.

Thus the word for one is *mei*, two is *bie*, three is *bei*, four *ban*, five *bolan*, six *bolanmei*, seven *bolanbie*, eight *bolanbei*, nine *bolanban*, and ten *da*.[45] Fathers are called *batuo*, and even paternal uncles are, too. Mothers are called *mi*, and so are paternal and maternal aunts and the wives of fathers' younger brothers, and even older women in the neighborhood. Elder brothers are called *bang*, and so are elder sisters. Younger brothers are called *buwen* and maternal uncles are called *chilai*, as are the husbands of paternal and maternal aunts.[46]

In general many of the words that come afterwards, they put in front. For example, we may say that that man is Zhang San's younger brother; they say he is "*buwen* Zhang San." We say that this man is Li Si's maternal uncle; they say he is "*chilai* Li Si."[47]

To give another example, China is called Beishi, an official is called *bading*, and a scholar is called *banjie*.[48] But a Chinese official isn't called Beishi *bading*; rather, he is called *bading* Beishi. And a Chinese scholar isn't called Beishi *banjie*; rather, he is called *banjie* Beishi. On the whole, it is all like that.

This is just a brief general outline. When it comes to specifics, officialdom has its official debates and deliberations, scholars have their scholarly literary conversations, and the Buddhists and Daoists have their own languages of Buddhism and Daoism. The towns and villages all have their own particular ways of speaking—but then again, that is no different from China.

~: :~

11
SAVAGES

There are two kinds of savage. The first know how to deal with people and talk to them, and are sold into the towns as slaves. The second are uneducated and cannot communicate in words.

This second kind have no homes to live in, but move from place to place in the mountains, taking their family with them and carrying a clay pot on their head as they walk. When they come across a wild animal they shoot it with a bow and arrow, then take it, make a fire by striking stones, roast it, and eat it together before setting off again. By nature they are very ferocious; their herbal concoctions are highly poisonous; and within their own groups they frequently kill one another.[49]

On land that is closer by there are also some who grow cardamom and kapok and weave cloth for a living, but the cloth is very coarse and thick, and the floral designs on it are very odd-looking.[50]

~: :~

12
WRITING

Everyday writing and official documents are all done on the skin of muntjaks, deer, etc., that is dyed black.[51] Depending on whether it is big or small, broad or narrow, the skin is cut in whatever way is desired. People use a kind of powder like Chinese chalk, which is rolled into a little stick called *suo* and held between forefinger and thumb, to draw shapes on the parchment and make words.[52] These stay fast forever. When they have finished with the chalk they stick it behind their ear. From the form of the words people can also make out whose handwriting it is. It can only be erased by being wiped with something wet.

For the most part the shape of the words is just like the shape of words written in Uighur.[53] The writing is always from left to right, not from top to bottom. I have heard Esen Khaya say that the letters of the alphabet are pronounced in exactly the same way as in Mongolian, with two or three exceptions.[54]

Official seals are non-existent. For families petitioning the authorities there are no shops with writers for hire, either.[55]

~: ~

13

NEW YEAR AND OTHER TIMES OF YEAR

The first month of the year is always the tenth month of the Chinese calendar. The month is called *Jiade*.[56] A large stage is set up in front of the royal palace. There is room on it for a thousand or more people. It is hung everywhere with globe lanterns and flowers. Facing it on a bank more than two or three hundred feet away are some tall structures that are made of wood joined and bound together, like the scaffolding used to make a pagoda.[57] They must be well over two hundred feet high. Every night they put up three or four of these, or five or six of them, and set out fireworks and firecrackers on top of them. The various provincial officials and great houses take care of all the costs.[58]

When night comes the king is invited to come out and watch. He lights the fireworks and firecrackers—the fireworks can all be seen a hundred *li* away. The firecrackers are as big as the rocks thrown by trebuchets and make enough noise to shake the whole city.[59] All the officials and members of the royal family give their share of huge candles and betel nuts, and spend a very great deal. The king also invites foreign envoys as spectators. Things go on in this way for fifteen days before coming to an end.

Every month there is always an event. For example, in the fourth month there are ball games. In the ninth month there is "ya lie."[60] *Ya lie* involves everyone in the country gathering together in the capital and being reviewed in front of the palace. In the fifth month there is "water to welcome the Buddha," when Buddhas throughout the country, far and near, are all brought together and taken into the water, where they are bathed in the company of the king. There is also "dry land boating," which the king goes up a tower to watch.

The seventh month is the time for "rice burning," when new rice that is ready for harvesting is ceremoniously received outside the south gate, and burned as an offering to all the Buddhas. Countless women in chariots and on elephants come and watch, though the king does not appear.

In the eighth month there is "*ailan*," a dance that selected female dancers perform daily in the palace. There are boar fights and elephant fights as well, and again the king invites foreign envoys as spectators. Things go on like this for ten days.[61]

The events of the other months I cannot record in detail.

In this country there are also people who are expert astronomers. They can predict all the partial eclipses of the sun and the moon. But their long and short months are quite different from China's. Like China they have years with intercalary months, but they only intercalate a ninth month, which I cannot understand at all. They divide the night into only four watches; and every seven days is a cycle, similar in kind to China's so-called "open, shut . . . set up, take away" cycle of twelve days.[62]

Since none of the locals has a surname or given name, they don't keep a record of their birthdays. Many of them call themselves by the name of the day they were born on. Two days in their cycle are the luckiest;

three days are ordinary; and four are the most unlucky. Which day you can travel east on, which day you can go west on—even the women all know how to work these out.

Their twelve calendar animals are also the same as China's, only they call them by different names. So for example horse is *bu sai*, rooster is *luan*, pig is *zhilu*, and ox is *ge*.[63]

~: :~

14
SETTLING DISPUTES

If there is a dispute among the ordinary people, it must be referred up to the king, even if it is a small matter. There are never any whippings or floggings as punishment, only fines as I have heard. Nor do they hang or behead anyone guilty of a serious crime. Instead they just dig a ditch in the ground outside the west gate of the city, put the criminal inside it, fill it up solid with earth and stones, and leave it at that. Otherwise people have their fingers or toes amputated, or their nose cut off.

There is, however, no prohibition against adultery or gambling. If a husband finds out that his wife has committed adultery, he has her lover's feet squeezed between two pieces of wood. When he is unable to bear the pain the lover gives the husband everything he owns, and only then can he get his release. Given this practice, sometimes things are set up so as to defraud people.

If a person finds a dead body by his doorway, he himself drags it with a rope to wasteland outside the city. There is never anything that could be called an inquest or official inspection.

When a family catches a thief, they can also impose their own punishment, whether it is detention, torture, or beating. There is however one standard process for the use of, say, a family that has lost something and suspects it has been stolen by someone who won't own up. They heat some oil in a cauldron until it is extremely hot, and make the person concerned put their hand in it. If they are the thief, their hand turns putrid; if they are not, their skin and flesh stay the same as before. Such are the strange laws of foreigners.

Then again, if two families have a dispute to resolve and cannot agree on right and wrong, there are twelve small stone towers [Prasat Suor Prat] on a bank opposite the palace, and the two people concerned are sent to sit in two of them.[64] Outside, members of each family keep guard against the other. They may sit in the towers for a day or two, or for three or four days. Then for sure the one who is in the wrong becomes visibly ill, and leaves. He may have sores, or a cough or fever or something of the kind. The one who is in the right is absolutely fine. Thus right and wrong are assessed and decided on, in what is known as the judgment of heaven. Such is the spiritual power of the local gods.

~: :~

15
LEPROSY AND OTHER ILLNESSES

The people of this country are frequently ill, and can often cure themselves by immersing themselves in water and repeatedly washing their head. At the same time there are a lot of lepers—they are everywhere on the roads—and local people think nothing of sleeping and eating in their company. They sometimes say the disease occurs because of particular local conditions. It is also said that a king once contracted the disease, so people are not troubled by it.[65]

In my humble opinion people contract the disease because they so often go into the water and bathe after making love. I have heard that local people always go and bathe as soon as their love-making is over.

Out of every ten people that contract dysentery, eight or nine die.

They have people who sell medicines in the markets, as with us, but the medicines are not the same as the ones in China, and I do not know what they are made of.

There are also witchdoctors of some kind that give people their help. It's really most amusing.

∾ ∾

16
DEATH

When people die there are no coffins. The body is just kept on a kind of bamboo mat and covered with a cloth. When it is taken out for the funeral it is preceded by banners, drums, and music, as with us. Two dishes are filled with fried rice, and this is scattered along the route. The body is carried out of town to a remote, uninhabited spot, where it is thrown down and left. After that, vultures, crows, dogs, and other village animals come and eat it.[66] If it is quickly consumed, that means the father and mother of the dead person are blessed and so gained this reward. If it is not eaten or only partly eaten, on the other hand, it means the father and mother have come to this pass because of their wrongdoings.

Nowadays there are also more and more cremations, mainly of the offspring of Chinese.

When a father or mother dies, there are no special clothes for mourning. Sons show their respect for their parent by shaving off all their hair, daughters by shaving a space the size of a coin in the hair on the top of their head.

The kings are still buried in towers, though I do not know if their corpses are buried or just their bones.[67]

~: :~

17
CULTIVATING THE LAND

In general crops can be harvested three or four times a year, the reason being that all four seasons are like our fifth and sixth months, with days that know no frost or snow. For six months the land has rain, for six months no rain at all. From the fourth to the ninth month it rains every day, with the rain falling in the afternoon. The high water mark around the Freshwater Sea [Tonle Sap Lake] can reach some seventy or eighty feet, completely submerging even very tall trees except for the tips. Families living by the shore all move to the far side of the hills.[68]

From the tenth to the third month there is not a drop of rain. Only small boats can cross the Sea, whose lower depths are no more than three to five feet down.[69] The families move back down again, and the farmers work out when the paddy will be ripe and when the waters will have spread where, and sow their seed accordingly.

For plowing they do not use cows. Their plows, sickles, and hoes are quite similar to ours, but of course they are not made the same way.

There is also a kind of uncultivated field, where rice usually grows even though it is not planted. If the water in the field gets to be ten feet high, the rice grows at that height too. I assume this is a different variety of rice.

They do not use nightsoil for manuring the fields or growing vegetables, thinking it unclean.[70] Chinese who come to Cambodia never talk to people about matters relating to manure and fertilizer, for fear of being looked down on.

To make a latrine, groups of two or three families get together and dig a hole, which they cover with grass. When it is used up they fill it in and dig another one. Whenever they go to the lavatory they always go and wash themselves in a pond afterwards. They only use their left hand, keeping their right hand for taking food. When they see a Chinese going to the lavatory and wiping himself with paper they all laugh at him, to the point where they don't want him in their home. Among the women there are some who also urinate standing up—and that really is funny.

~: :~

18

THE LANDSCAPE

Coming up from Zhenpu, you skirt many tree-covered plains and forests, going several hundred *li* to traverse the huge estuary of the long river from one end to the other.[71] Birds and animals make a riot of sound in the dark, shadowy forests with their old trees and tall bamboos.[72] Halfway across the estuary you start to see spacious fields completely bare of trees. As far as the eye can see there is nothing but a thick, matted carpet of millet. Herds of wild buffalo, countless thousands strong, gather there.[73]

There are also slopes of bamboo stretching hundreds of *li* from end to end. Thorns grow in the joints of the bamboo, and the bamboo shoots have a most bitter taste.

On all four sides there are high mountains.[74]

~: :~

19

PRODUCTS

In the mountains there are exotic trees in plenty. Where there are no trees, rhinos and elephants come together and bring up their young. There are precious birds and wonderful animals too numerous to count. Fine things include kingfisher feathers, elephant tusks, rhinoceros horns, and beeswax. Less refined things include rosewood, cardamom, gamboge, lac, and chaulmoogra oil.

Kingfishers are really quite hard to catch. Where there is a lake in a forest and there are fish in the lake, the kingfisher flies out of the trees in search of them. The locals cover their bodies with leaves and sit by the edge of a lake, where they catch a female kingfisher in a cage as a lure for the males. They wait for the males to come, then trap them with a small hand-held net. Sometimes they take three to five birds in a day; sometimes they get absolutely nothing all day.

Elephant tusks come from families living in remote mountain areas. When any elephant dies it still has its two tusks; there is no truth in the old saying that elephants change their tusks each year. The best ivory comes from elephants killed with a lance; the next best, from those whose tusks people have collected soon after they have died a natural death; the least good, from those that have been lying dead in the mountains for many years.

The locals get beeswax from a kind of bee with a narrow waist like an ant's that lives inside rotten trees in the villages. Every junk can carry two or three thousand honeycombs of beeswax, and each comb weighs between forty and fifty-five pounds for a large one, and twenty-five or twenty-six pounds for a small one.

Better-quality rhino horns are white with veining; the less good ones are dark.

Rosewood grows in the forest. The locals expend a great deal of effort breaking and cutting up the trees, as the wood comes from the heart of the trees. They are white on the outside and about eight or nine inches thick. Even the small ones are no less than four or five inches thick. Cardamom is cultivated entirely by the savages in the mountains. Gamboge is resin from a kind of tree. The locals cut the tree with a knife a year in advance, letting the resin drip out, then start collecting it a year later. Lac grows on the branches of a kind of tree, looks just like mulberry mistletoe, and is also quite hard to obtain. Chaulmoogra oil comes from the seeds of a large tree. The fruit is round and shaped like a coconut; inside there are several dozen seeds.[75]

In some places there are also peppers. They grow on a twisting vine that forms clusters like wild hops. When they are fresh the dark green ones are hotter than the others.[76]

～: ～

20
TRADE

The local people who know how to trade are all women. So when a Chinese goes to this country, the first thing he must do is take in a woman, partly with a view to profiting from her trading abilities.

There is a market every day from around six in the morning until midday. There are no stalls, only a kind of tumbleweed mat laid out on the ground, each mat in its usual place. I gather there is also a rental fee to be paid to officials.

Small market transactions are paid for with rice or other grain and Chinese goods. The ones next up in size are paid for with cloth. Large transactions are done with gold and silver.

In years gone by local people were completely naïve, and when they saw a Chinese they treated him with great respect and awe, addressing him as a Buddha and falling prostrate and kowtowing when they saw him. Lately, though, as more Chinese have gone there, there have been people who have cheated and slighted them.

~: :~

21
SOUGHT-AFTER CHINESE GOODS

They do not produce gold or silver in Cambodia, I believe, and so they hold Chinese gold and silver in the highest regard.

Next they value items made of fine, double-threaded silk in various colors.[77] Next after that they value such things as pewter ware from Zhenzhou, lacquer dishes from Wenzhou, and celadon ware from Quanzhou and Chuzhou,[78] as well asmercury, cinnabar, writing paper, sulphur, saltpeter, sandalwood, lovage, angelica, musk, hemp, yellow grasscloth, umbrellas, iron pots, copper dishes, glass balls, tung tree oil, fine-toothed combs, wooden combs, and needles—and of the ordinary, heavier items, mats from Mingzhou. Beans and wheat are particularly sought after, but they cannot be taken there.[79]

~: :~

22
FLORA

All they have in common with China are pomegranates, sugarcane, lotus flowers, lotus roots, Chinese gooseberries, and bananas. Their lychees and oranges are the same shape as ours, but they have a sour taste. The rest are all things we in China have never seen. And their trees really are very different from ours, while their grasses and flowers are fragrant and beautiful and more plentiful than ours. There are also more varieties of aquatic flowers, though I do not know any of their names.

As for peaches, plums, apricots, flowering apricots, pines, cypresses, firs, junipers, pears, jujubes, poplars, willows, cassias, orchids, chrysanthemums, and angelica—these they have none of. They do have lotus flowers in the first month of the year, though.[80]

~: :~

23
BIRDS

Of their birds, peacocks, kingfishers, and parrots do not exist in China. Otherwise they have birds like vultures, crows, egrets, sparrows, great cormorants, storks, cranes, wild ducks, siskins, etc.[81] They don't have magpies, wild geese, orioles, cuckoos, swallows, or pigeons.

~: :~

24
ANIMALS

Of their animals, rhinos, elephants, wild buffalo, and mountain horses do not exist in China. Otherwise they have very many kinds of animals, including tigers, leopards, different kinds of bear, wild boar, elk, deer, water deer, muntjaks, apes, foxes, and gibbons. The only animals that aren't seen are lions, orangutans, and camels. And of course there are chickens, ducks, cows, horses, pigs, and goats.

The horses are very short and small. There are a great many cows. People do not venture to ride on them when they are alive, or eat them when they are dead, or flay their hides for leather, and—I hear—their carcasses are left to rot away, all because they exert their best efforts for people. They are used to haul carts and nothing else.[82]

Originally there were no geese, but in recent times sailors from China brought them into the country, so now they are being raised.

They have rats as large as cats; there is also a kind of rat whose head looks exactly like a newborn puppy's.

∼: ∼

25
VEGETABLES

For vegetables they have onions, mustard, chives, eggplants, watermelons, winter gourds, snake gourds, and amaranth.[83] They do not have radishes, lettuce, chicory, or spinach.[84] Watermelons, gourds, and eggplants are also available in some places as early as the second month of the year. Some eggplants can be left for several years without being uprooted.

There are silk cotton trees higher than a room that are not replaced for more than ten years at a time.[85]

There are very many vegetables whose names I don't know. There are also many kinds of vegetables that grow in water.

∼: ∼

26
FISH AND REPTILES

Of their fish and turtles, black carp are the commonest. Other fish that are plentiful include common carp, goldfish, and grass carp. There are gudgeons—the large ones weigh up to three pounds.[86] Otherwise there are very many fish whose names I don't know, all of them coming from the Freshwater Sea.[87]

As for saltwater fish, they have every different kind.

There are also swamp eels and the freshwater eels from the lakes. The local people do not eat frogs, which go this way and that across the roads at night.

There are giant soft-shell turtles and alligators as big as large pillars. The turtles are served up offal and all. Prawns from Zhanan weigh a pound and a half or more each. The goose-necked barnacles from Zhenpu may be eight or nine inches long.[88]

There are crocodiles as big as boats. They have four feet and look exactly like dragons except they have no horns.

The razor clams look very fine and are very crisp-tasting. They get clams, mud clams, and pond snails by just scooping them out of the Freshwater Sea. The only things I did not see were crabs. They do have crabs, I believe, but people don't eat them.

~: ~

27
FERMENTED LIQUOR

They have four kinds of wine. The first is what the Chinese call "honey-sweet wine," made by mixing a fermenting agent into honey and water. The next, which the local people call *pengyasi*, is made from the leaves of a kind of tree, the leaves being known by that name. The third is made from husked rice, or rice left over after a meal. It is called *baolengjiao*, which means husked rice. The last is "sugar-shine wine," which is made from sugar. Down by the banks of the estuary they also have a palm starch wine, which they make from the starch of the leaves of a type of palm that grows on the riverbank.[89]

~: :~

28

SALT, VINEGAR, AND SOY SAUCE

There is no prohibition on salt works in the country, and from Zhenpu to Bajian and other locations along the coast, most places heat seawater to make salt. In the mountains there is also a kind of rock that tastes even better than salt, and that can be carved into objects.[90]

The local people cannot make vinegar. If they want to give a sauce a sour taste they add some leaves from the tamarind tree—or berries from the tree if it has produced berries, or seeds from the trees if it has produced seeds.[91]

They do not know how to make soy sauce, either. This is because they have no soy beans or wheat, and have never made a fermenting agent. So they make wine from honey, water, and the leaves of a tree, and use a wine yeast that looks like the spirit yeast used in our villages.[92]

~: :~

29

SILK PRODUCTION

None of the locals produces silk. Nor do the women know how to stitch and darn with a needle and thread. The only thing they can do is weave cotton from kapok. Even then they cannot spin the yarn, but just use their hands to gather the cloth into strands. They do not use a loom for weaving. Instead they just wind one end of the cloth around their waist, hang the other end over a window, and use a bamboo tube as a shuttle.

In recent years people from Siam have come to live in Cambodia, and unlike the locals they engage in silk production. The mulberry trees they grow and the silkworms they raise all come from Siam. (They have no ramie, either, only hemp.)[93] They themselves weave the silk into clothes made of a black, patterned satiny silk. Siamese women do know how to stitch and darn, so when local people have torn or damaged clothing they ask them to do the mending.

~: :~

30
UTENSILS

Ordinary families have houses but nothing else by way of tables, chairs, jars, or buckets. They use an earthenware pot to cook rice in, and make sauce with an earthenware saucepan. For a stove they sink three stones into the ground, and for spoons they use coconut husks.

When serving rice they use earthenware or copper dishes from China; sauce comes in a small bowl made from the leaves of a tree, which doesn't leak even when it is full of liquid. They also make small spoons from the leaves of the nypa palm, which they spoon liquid into their mouths with, and throw away after using. Even when they are making offerings to the gods and to the Buddha, they do things the same way.

They also have a tin or earthenware vessel on one side which they fill with water and dip their hands in. They do this because they eat rice with just their hands, and it sticks to their hands and won't come off without water.

When they drink wine they do so from a pewter vessel called a *qia* that holds about three or four small cupfuls. When serving wine they do so with a pewter pot, though poor people use a clay jug.[94] In the great houses and wealthy homes, silver or even gold is used for everything. In the palace they often use receptacles of gold, different from the others in style and shape.

On the ground they lay out grass mats from Mingzhou, or rattan matting, or the pelts of tigers, leopards, muntjaks, deer, and so on.[95] Lately people have started using low tables, about a foot high. When they sleep they just lie on the ground on bamboo mats. Lately, again, they have taken to using low beds, usually made by Chinese.

At night there are a lot of mosquitoes, so they use cloth nets. In the king's quarters the nets are made of fine silk with gold filigree work, all of them the gifts of seafaring merchants.

For husking rice they don't use millstones, just pestle and mortar.

~: :~

31
CARTS AND PALANQUINS

Their palanquins are made of pieces of wood that bend in the middle and point upward at either end. They are carved with floral designs and girdled with gold or silver, which is what I meant by gold and silver palanquin poles.[96]

One foot down from each end of the palanquin pole is a hook nailed into the wood. A large cloth folded thick is tied to the hooks with a rope. A person sits in the cloth and is carried by two people, one at either end. In addition palanquins come with a thing like the sail of a boat, except broader, which is decorated with fine silk done in many colors. It is carried by four men, who follow along with it.

For long distances they also ride on elephants and horses, or use carts. The carts are made in the same way as in other places, but the horses have no saddles. The elephants, on the other hand, carry benches to sit on.

~: ~

32
BOATS

Very large boats are made from hardwood broken into planks. The carpenters have no saws, and just chisel the wood with axes so as to make the planks. This is very cumbersome, a waste of wood, and a waste of effort. For anything needing wood cut into lengths, including house building, the wood is chiseled and cut into pieces in the same way. To make the boats they also use iron nails. The awning consists of palm leaves held down with strips of areca wood. They use oars for these boats, which they call *xinna*. The grease they spread on them is fish oil, and they use lime for mortar.

Small boats, on the other hand, are made from a single very large piece of wood, hollowed out by chiseling. They treat the wood with smoke from a fire, which makes it soft, then use timber to stretch it out. The boats, which they call *pilan*, are large in the middle and pointed at either end. They don't have a sail, can hold several people, and have to be rowed with oars.[97]

~: ~

33
PREFECTURES

The country has ninety or so prefectures. There are Zhenpu, Zhanan, Bajian, Moliang, Baxue, Pumai, Zhigun, Mujinbo, Laigankeng, and Basili. I cannot record all the others. They all have their officials, and they all have walls consisting of wooden stockades.[98]

~: :~

34
VILLAGES

In every village there is a Buddhist temple or a pagoda. Where the population is quite dense there is normally an official called *maijie* who is responsible for the security of the village. Resting places called *senmu*, like our posting-houses, are normally found along the main roads.

As a result of repeated wars with the Siamese the land has been completely laid to waste.[99]

~: :~

35
TAKING GALL

Previously, gall bladders were taken from people in the eighth month in response to an annual demand from the king of Champa for an urn filled with human gall bladders—perhaps a thousand or more of them. At night men were sent out in many directions to well-frequented places in towns and villages. When they met people out at night they snared their head with a rope and took out their gall bladder by sticking a small knife into their lower right-hand side. When there were enough of these they were given to the Champa king.

The only gall bladders they did not take were those of Chinese, since one year they took one from a Chinese and put it in with the others, only to find that the gall bladders in the urn all turned rotten and could not be used.

Recently the practice of taking gall bladders has been done away with. The officials who took the gall bladders have been reassigned, and reside inside the north gate of the city.[100]

~: :~

36
A STRANGE AFFAIR

Inside the east gate there was a barbarian who had sex with his younger sister.[101] Their skin and flesh stuck together and would not come apart. After three days without eating they both died. My fellow countryman Mr. Xue has lived in this place for thirty-five years, and says he has seen this same thing happen twice.[102] Such then is the spiritual power of the holy Buddha in this country.

~: :~

37
BATHING

The place is unbearably hot, and no one can go on without bathing several times a day. Even at night you have to bathe once or twice. They may never have had bathrooms, buckets, or the like, but every family is sure to have a pool, or at least a pool to share among two or three families.

Everyone, male and female, goes naked into the pool. The only exceptions are when there are parents or elderly people in the pool, in which case children and youngsters do not venture in, or when there are young people in the pool, in which case elderly people have to stay away too. For people from the same generation there are no constraints, though women do cover their vagina with their left hand when they go into the water.

Every three or four days, or every four or five days, women in the capital get together in groups of three to five and go out of the city to bathe in the river. When they get to the riverside they take off the cloth they are wrapped in and go into the water. Those gathering together in the river often number in thousands. Even the women from the great houses join in, without the slightest embarrassment. You get to see everything, from head to toe.

In the big river outside the city not a day passes without this happening. On their leisure days Chinese regard it as quite a pleasant thing to go along and watch; and I have heard that there are those who go into the water for a surreptitious encounter.

The river is always warm, like heated water. Only in the fifth watch does it get a little cooler. But as soon as the sun appears it warms up again.[103]

∾: ∿

38
LIVING ABROAD

Chinese sailors do well by the fact that in this country you can go without clothes, food is easy to come by, women are easy to get, housing is easy to deal with, it is easy to make do with a few utensils, and it is easy to do trade. They often run away here.

∾: ∿

39

THE ARMY

The soldiers, too, go naked and barefoot. In their right hand they carry a lance, and in their left hand a shield. They have nothing that could be called bows and arrows, trebuchets, body armor, helmets, or the like.[104]

I have heard reports that when the Siamese attacked, all the ordinary people were ordered out to do battle, often with no good strategy or preparation.

~: :~

40

THE KING IN AND OUT OF THE PALACE

I have heard that during the time of the last king, there were no chariot tracks in and out of the palace, so concerned was he to guard against unforeseen events. The new king is the old king's son-in-law.[105] Originally he was in charge of the soldiers. When his father-in-law died his wife secretly stole the gold sword and gave it to him.[106] The old king's own son was thus deprived of the succession. The son then planned a military uprising, but the new king found out about it, cut off his toes, and put him away in a dark room. The new king had a sacred piece of iron embedded in his body, so that if anything like a knife or an arrow touched him he could not be injured. With this to rely on he ventured to come out of the palace.

I stayed for a year or so, and saw him come out four or five times. Each time he came out all his soldiers were gathered in front of him, with people bearing banners, musicians, and drummers following behind him. One contingent was made up of three to five hundred women of the palace. They wore clothes with a floral design and flowers in their coiled-up hair, and carried huge candles, alight even though it was daylight. There were also women of the palace carrying gold and silver utensils from the palace and finely decorated instruments made in exotic and unusual styles, for what purpose I do not know. Palace women carrying lances and shields made up another contingent as the palace guard. Then there were carts drawn by goats, deer, and horses, all of them decorated with gold.

All the ministers, officials, and relatives of the king were in front, riding elephants.[107] Their red parasols, too many to number, were visible in the distance. Next came the king's wives and concubines and their servants, some in palanquins and carts, others on horses or elephants, with well over a hundred gold filigree parasols. Last came the king, standing on an elephant, the gold sword in his hand and the tusks of his elephant encased in gold. He had more than twenty white parasols decorated with gold filigree, their handles all made of gold. Surrounding him on all four sides were elephants in very large numbers, with soldiers to protect him as well.

If he was going to a place nearby, the king just rode on a gold palanquin carried by palace women. He only used a gold cart, I heard, if the place he was visiting was quite a distance away.[108]

Generally when leaving or returning to the palace he had to visit a small gold stupa, with a gold Buddha in front of it. Onlookers all had to kneel down and touch their head on the ground in a gesture called *sanba*. If they did not they were arrested by officers of protocol, who did not lightly release them.[109]

Twice a day the king sat in his outer palace and dealt with matters of government, and did so without anything fixed in writing.[110] All the ministers and ordinary people that wanted to see him sat in a row on the ground and waited for him. After a while you heard the muffled sound of music from the inner palace, while outside a conch shell blew to welcome him. In a moment you saw the delicate hands of two palace women rolling up a curtain to reveal the king, sword in hand, standing framed in a golden window. Ministers, officials, and people of lower rank all put their hands together in greeting and bowed to the ground. They were only allowed to lift their head when the sound of the conch stopped. The king then proceeded to sit down. I heard that where he sat there was a lion skin, a national treasure he had inherited.

When he had finished speaking about official matters, the king at once turned away. Two palace women lowered the curtain again, and everyone rose.

We can see from this that although this is a country of barbarians, they all know at first hand that they have a supreme ruler.[111]

~: :~

NOTES

General Preface

1. In Chinese versions of this book the title is followed by the name of the author and a few words about him. He is described as Zhou Daguan of the Yuan dynasty, from Yongjia 永嘉. The work of dividing the book into sections with titles may have been done by later editors, though this remains in doubt. The section numbers, which I have called chapter numbers, may also be later additions. For section titles, see XN, 197–198.

The "sacred dynasty" is the Mongol Yuan 元 dynasty in China. The "Buddhist scriptures of the Tibetans" are actually described in the text as "the scriptures of the western foreigners (*xi fan jing* 西番經)." As Pelliot argues, the scriptures are clearly the Buddhist canon; and given Mongol rule in China, the term *xi fan* or "western foreigners" could as easily refer to Tibetans as to central Asians or Indians. Tibetan Buddhism had a strong influence on Khubilai Khan and the Mongol court, though Tibetan literature itself makes no mention of Cambodia until centuries later. For more on these topics, see CHC, 416–417, 460–461; Rossabi, *Khubilai Khan, His Life and Times*, 192–198; pp, 83.

No one knows for certain why Cambodia was once called Zhenla 真臘. One explanation is that the name means "Defeated Siam." At first sight, this makes some sense given the pronunciation of Zhenla when the name first came into use in the seventh century CE (Tsienliäp, to give Karlgren's Tang dynasty pronunciation; by Zhou's time the pronunciation was closer to Tsinla, the Yuan dynasty sound as reconstructed by Pulleyblank). Tsienliäp bears some resemblance to the name Siem Reap, the present-day town near Angkor, which nowadays is widely taken to mean "Defeated Siam" (literally, "Flattened Siam" or possibly "Siam Flattened"). Unfortunately this explanation is vitiated by the fact that hostilities between Cambodia and Siam—precursor to present-day Thailand—seem to have taken place many centuries after the name Zhenla was first used. Moreover Michael Vickery argues convincingly that the interpretation of Siem Reap as "flattened Siam" is modern folk etymology, and argues that while the two names Zhenla and Siem Reap may perhaps be related, the original meanings of both names is as yet unknown. Vickery, *Society, Economics and Politics in Pre-Angkor Cambodia*, 421; LR 401, 181; GSR 107, 169.

The variant form Zhanla 占臘 is easier to explain. It very likely means "Defeated Chams," since Zhan 占 is the word in Chinese for Cham. Given the persistent hostility between Cambodians and Chams, vividly illustrated by the fighting scenes on the reliefs at Bayon, this explanation makes good sense. It is the explanation for Zhanla given in *Ming shi*, the official Chinese history of the Ming dynasty. *Ming shi* recounts: "During the *qingyuan* reign period (1195–1200) of the Song dynasty, Cambodia wiped out Champa and took over its land. Because of this, the country changed its name to Zhanla. But during the Yuan dynasty it went on being called Zhenla." *Ming shi, juan* 324, 8394. On the meanings of Zhenla and Zhanla, see XN, 16–18; PP, 71–82.

Ganpuzhi 澉浦只 and Ganbozhi 甘孛智 are Chinese renderings of the Sanskrit name Kambuja, which is the basis of the name Cambodians use today. In Cambodian mythology, Kambuja was named after the founding ancestor, Kambu, an Indian who arrived by ship, married the daughter of a local serpent king, and founded a dynasty with her. This myth may explain the story of the Cambodian king's nightly coupling with a serpent spirit that is recounted in chapter 2. The Cambodians began using the name Kambuja in the eighth century, and the Chinese began employing it, or at least Chinese versions of it, from Yuan times on. The name is used at least once in *Yuan shi*. However it was not until the Wanli period of the Ming dynasty (1573–1619) that the Chinese officially changed the name they used for Cambodia from Zhenla to Jianpuzhai 柬埔寨, a transliteration of Kambuja still used by Beijing today. For details, see XN, 39; CH, 368; *Ming shi, juan* 324, 8396; Vickery, *Society, Economics and Politics in Pre-Angkor Cambodia*, 420–421; Jacques, *Angkor*, 376, as quoted in Chandler, *A History of Cambodia*, 26.

Except for here in the preface and in chapter 1, Zhou never uses the term Zhenla or any other proper nouns for Cambodia. Instead he refers to the country indirectly through the use of pronouns and adjectives such as *qi* 其. In all such cases I have used the term Cambodia.

2. I have given the compass points in north-south-east-west terms, but Zhou actually names two of the points on a 24-division compass, *dingwei* 丁未 and *kunshen* 坤申. These are shown in map 2. Compasses in China date back to Han dynasty times, as shown by the compasses found in Han dynasty graves, and sophisticated magnetic compasses with 24 divisions were in regular use in Zhou's time. On compasses in Han tombs, see XN, 23. On 24-division compasses, see J. Needham, *Science and Civilization in China,Volume 4, Physics and Physical Technology, Part 1* (Cambridge: Cambridge University Press, 1962), 279–293.

Min 閩 and Guang 廣 were regions covering most of southeastern China. Min is generally associated with the present-day province of Fujian and Guang with the present-day province of Guangdong and nearby locations. In Yuan times Min and Guang consisted of parts of the then provinces of Jiangzhe 江浙, Jiangxi 江西; and Huguang 湖廣. See F. W. Mote, *Imperial China, 900–1800* (Cambridge: Harvard University Press, 1999), 486.

The "various overseas ports" seem to have been places in Hainan Island, and possibly on the south coast of the mainland as well. The text actually reads "the various *zhou* 州 ports overseas."

The Seven Islands Sea (*Qi Zhou Yang* 七洲洋) was a name commonly used for the part of the South China Sea nearest China. To this day a cluster of small islands east of Hainan Island is called the Seven Islands (Qi Zhou 七洲). The South China Sea was hard to navigate, judging from a Ming dynasty sailors' jingle quoted in CH, 31:

> *Beware the Seven Isles up north*
> *And southward Kunlun too.*
> *Your compass spins, your rudder's lost*
> *And you and the boat are through.*

From the second century CE on, Jiaozhi [P Kjawtsr, K Kaotsi] 交趾 was a name often used to describe the area near present-day Hanoi. LRP, 150, 407; GSR, 300, 253. The Jiaozhi Sea (交趾洋) is thus today's Tongking Gulf, east of Hanoi. The kingdom of Champa (which Zhou and others at the time refer to as Zhancheng 占城, Cham City) was centered on the southeastern coast of Vietnam.

It is only possible to guess at the location of Zhenpu 真蒲, evidently somewhere along the coast of what is today the southern part of Vietnam, perhaps in the region of Vung Tau. Zhou mentions Zhenpu again in chapter 18, when he describes the Mekong estuary in more detail, and again in chapters 26 and 27, when he writes about its shellfish delicacies and salt works.

At the end of the paragraph, a textual variant has an additional sentence, which reads: "To the south of it there is a large river with an 浂 water—an means warm water" (see XN, 22–23). The sentence could be referring to the Mekong River, but it seems out of the place here.

Zhou uses the customary Chinese lunar calendar, which has 12 months in the year, alternately 29 and 30 days long. Here as elsewhere he writes "half a month," but this sounds awkward in English, and I have translated half a month as 15 days instead.

In the early part of the preface Zhou is clearly writing from his own experience, even though he does not say so. It is only toward the end of the preface that he introduces the personal pronoun "I," a word he does not often use. The practice of writing "I" and "me" was less common in the literary Chinese of Zhou's day than it is in modern English. Thus, as noted in the introduction, it is sometimes hard to know how personal Zhou's observations are. Sometimes Zhou helps us by distinguishing between what he has seen himself and what he has learned secondhand, remarking that he has "heard" something is so, or even specifying that he has not seen it with his own eyes.

3. The locations Zhou visits en route to the Cambodian capital are sometimes easy to identify, sometimes not. The Kunlun Sea 崑崙洋 is the part of the South China Sea beyond the mouth of the Mekong. (It was the second place mentioned in the sailors' saying quoted above.) There are some ten small islands near the mouth of the Mekong that are still known to the Chinese as the Kunlun Islands. The river with many estuaries is the Mekong.

4. Zhanan [ᴘ Tsanam, ᴋ Tsanam] 查南 is hard to pinpoint. Perhaps it is Kampong Chhnang, the present-day town beyond the southern end of Tonle Sap Lake, since its old pronunciation in Chinese, Tsanam, may resemble Chhnang. Zhou mentions Zhanan again in chapter 26 as the best place to get large prawns. ɢsʀ, 46 (variants), 650.

Zhou writes that Zhanan was a *jun* 郡, here translated "prefecture," which is a word he uses again in chapter 33. By the time of the Yuan dynasty, *jun* was an archaic word, having been used in Tang and pre-Tang times in references to China's principal second tier of government, the one immediately below the level of the province. China's Mongol rulers maintained an equivalent system, but had come to use a different term. See also note 98. For details, see ᴄʜ, 1195–1996; Mote, *Imperial China*, 487.

The terms Halfway Village and Buddha Village (Banlu Cun 半路村 and Fo Cun 佛村) may be descriptive or they may be proper names. We can be surer of Freshwater Sea (Dan Yang 淡洋, called Danshui Yang 淡水洋 in chapters 17 and 26), which is clearly the Tonle Sap Lake. Incidentally Tonle Sap is the only one of Zhou's names whose meaning comes close to that of the Cambodian name, since "Tonle Sap" means "Freshwater River" in Khmer.

Ganpang 干傍 is hard to identify. It could be the Khmer word that is usually written *kompong or kampong*, which originally may have meant pier or landing, and which is now found in many Cambodian place-names. Even so it is still not clear which town Zhou is referring to. (On the term *kompong* see Vickery, *Society, Economics and Politics in Pre-Angkor Cambodia*, 440–441.)

"... fifty *li* from the capital city": As noted in the introduction, a *li* 里 or Chinese mile as Zhou used it was probably the equivalent of half a kilometer or a third of an English mile (ᴄʜᴍ, 237). According to ᴄʜᴍ, 237, a *li* in Yuan times was actually one-third shorter than it was in Song and Ming times, but the Song value of the *li* corresponds better with actual lengths on the ground in Angkor and I am assuming that Zhou was still using it.

Given the short distance, Zhou must have taken a very slow boat from China to get from Zhenpu in southeastern Vietnam to the mouth of the Mekong in two weeks, especially with the wind behind him.

When Zhou writes about sailing up the Mekong "with a favorable current" he may have in mind—though he does notmention it—the remarkable fact that the waters of the Tonle Sap reverse their flows during the wet season, when the Mekong floods back up into the Tonle Sap and the Tonle Sap flows northwestward rather than in its usual southeastern direction. Zhou must have reached the Mekong in late June or early July, just as the rains were starting.

5. The *Treatise on the Various Foreigners*, or *Zhu fan zhi* 諸蕃志, is a thirteenth-century Chinese guide to the countries and peoples beyond China. Compiled by Zhao Rushi 趙汝適 in 1225, the original text of the *Treatise* was later lost, but a version of it was reproduced in the fifteenth-century *Yongle Encyclopedia* (Yongle Dadian 永樂大典). In the encyclopedia version the *Treatise* records that Cambodia "may be some 7,000 *li* square (*yue fang qi qian yu li* 約方七千餘里)," that is, square in shape with each length of the square measuring 7,000 li. This is consistent with what Zhou writes. If one *li* was about half a kilometer, the figure is far too large, many times the size of present-day Cambodia, which is about 181,000 square kilometers. If the meaning of the *Treatise text* is actually that the size of Cambodia is 7,000 square li, say 70 times 100 li, the figure is much too small, unless it refers only to the size of the capital. However *fang* 方 is not known to have been used in this latter sense of square in Yuan times. On Zhao Rushi: CH, 5084. On the *Treatise text*: XN, 35. On li-kilometer equivalents, weights and measures used elsewhere in this text, and the variable and unpredictable nature of these weights and measures: CHM, 234–240. On the use of *fang*: CHM, 242.

In Zhou's discussion of the distances from Cambodia to its neighbors, he refers to distances from the state (*guo* 國), but it is not clear where his calculations start from. He seems to be referring to distances from the capital, so I have taken *guo* here to refer primarily to the capital city on which the state was centered.

Here and in chapter 3 the word I have translated as "Siam" is Xianluo 暹羅. Elsewhere (chapters 10, 29, 34, 39) Zhou uses the word Xian 暹, which I have also rendered as Siam. Xianluo is a name formed from the names of two states, Xian and Lavo (Luohu 羅斛 in Chinese), and only came into use some fifty years after Zhou's visit, when Lavo was taken over by Xian. So perhaps Zhou was still working on his book in his old age. Alternatively, of course, the text was amended after his death. See PP, 98; XN, 36, Coedès, The Indianized States of Southeast Asia, 235.

It is not possible to identify Fanyu 番禺, the place ten days' journey south, somewhere toward the Malayan peninsula. The sea to the east must be the South China Sea. Zhou neglects the fact that the state of Champa lies in between, but perhaps he was thinking of "the east" in terms of the Mekong.

6. According to the official history of the Yuan dynasty, Sodu 唆都 ran to ground the last members of the imperial family of the defeated Song dynasty, then became Khubilai Khan's highest official in South China. As noted in the introduction, he was decapitated in 1285 while leading a punitive war against the Chams, who were refusing to accept Mongol suzerainty.

In the text, which I have paraphrased at this point, Zhou describes the Chinese military commanders sent to Champa by rank, given in terms of their insignia and the men under their charge. In general, the insignia given to senior Chinese military commanders took the form of tallies—a miniature tiger or a piece of gold or silver—that were cut in two, one half being given to the commander himself and the other being kept in court. According to Zhou the first of the two men sent to Champa had "a tiger tally and ten thousand households," making him roughly the equivalent today of a general in charge of a division. The second had "a gold tally and a thousand households," the rough equivalent today of a colonel in charge of a regiment. The official Yuan history explains that during the Yuan period there were three main categories of senior commander, the first two being the ones Zhou mentions and the third being someone with a silver tally and a hundred households. Marco Polo argues that the decimal command system, with officers in charge of ten thousand men, a thousand men, and so on, made for quick and efficient decision making. Details from CH, 5237; XN, 38–39; Latham, *Marco Polo: The Travels*, 99–100.

Zhou's comment about Sodu, the general, and the commander has caused some confusion. Some commentators (XN for example, and initially PP, though he later had doubts) have read "this country," *benguo* 本國, which I have translated as "there," as meaning Cambodia. On the face of it this is a reasonable interpretation, and Zhou does use the term *benguo* for Cambodia in chapter 8. However, *Yuan shi* makes no mention of the death or capture in Cambodia of two army commanders of the kind Zhou describes, whereas it does mention the capture by the state of Champa of two commanders just as Zhou describes them. I infer from this that *benguo* refers here not to Cambodia but to Champa. *Yuan shi, juan* 210, 4660; XN, 38–40, 119–123.

7. Temür succeeded his grandfather in 1294 as the Chinese emperor Chengzong. The new emperor was a drunkard, like his grandfather, but was otherwise a less ambitious man, and he soon called off military campaigns planned against the Vietnamese and Japan. As I suggested in the introduction, Zhou's visit to Champa and Cambodia was consistent with the less aggressive style of Chengzong's foreign policy.

Imperial edict: Zhou's term is *zhao yu* 招諭. The similar term *zhao* 詔諭 is the term customarily used for edict. *Zhao* 招 by itself usually means "summons," as when summoning a subordinate state to send its tribute and tribute-bearers to the Chinese capital.

8. "... arrived in Cambodia": The text has only *zhi* 至, "arrived," and I have added the two words "in Cambodia." Likewise, there is no word for Cambodia in the final sentence of the preface, only *qi* 其, "its," leaving the point of reference to be inferred. Given these omissions and the earlier confusion over *benguo*, there are grounds for supposing that the text in the final couple of paragraphs has been corrupted.

"... left Mingzhou" and "... back at Mingzhou": The text refers initially to Mingzhou 明州 but then goes on to say that the travelers arrived "back at Siming," Siming 四明 being Mingzhou's other name at that time. Mingzhou is known today as Ningbo 寧波. It is not far from Hangzhou 航州 and, as noted in the introduction, has long been one of the principal coastal ports of southeast China.

For dates, I have kept Chinese year names and reign period names, particularly Yuanzhen 元貞 (Prime Loyalty, 1295–1297) and Dade 大德 (Great Virtue, 1297–1308). According to this passage, Zhou left Wenzhou on 24 March 1296. He reached Champa on 18 April 1296 and reached Cambodia at the beginning of August that year. He set sail for home again some time between 21 June and 20 July 1297, and arrived back in Mingzhou on 30 August 1297. Despite what he writes in chapter 40, where he mentions spending "a year or so" in Cambodia, he therefore seems to have spent just under a year in the country.

Chapter 1: The City and its Walls

9.   Zhou begins his description of Cambodia with the contours of the royal city, which is now known as Angkor Thom ("Great Angkor"). Zhou himself never gives a name to the city. When he was there it was evidently still known as Yasodharapura, the name given to it in the tenth century. On an inscription at the time mentioning Yasodharapura, see Higham, *The Civilization of Angkor*, 138.

Assuming Zhou Daguan was still using Song dynasty measurements, the *li* or Chinese mile was probably the equivalent of roughly half a kilometer or one-third of a mile. On the accuracy of Zhou's measurements, see note [17].

10. "On either side of every bridge" reads *ge* 各 for *gong* 共, in line with most versions of the text.

"Four of them face toward the four cardinal points" follows XN and PP and amends *xifang* 西方 "west" to *si fang* 四方 "the four cardinal directions."

The text is ambiguous as to whether all five of the heads above the gateways were decorated with gold, or only the middle one. Given their importance and what we read later about the quite widespread use of gold, it may be reasonable to assume that they were all decorated with gold. On the other hand the absence here of the word *jie* 皆 "all," a word often used by Zhou in such contexts to indicate that a description applies to all elements of the preceding noun or noun phrase, suggests that here the adjectival phrase "decorated with gold" refers only to the middle head. xn takes it that way.

Zhou's description of the four walls facing the cardinal points and five gates with elephants carved on to them conforms to what exists at Angkor Thom today. So does his description of the fifty-four stone figures pulling a snake on either side of the city bridges. (On a minor point of accuracy, he says they are all deities, though in fact twenty-seven of them are gods and twenty-seven of them demons.) However, the bridges are now solid structures, with no arches for water to flow under them, and the snakes or *naga* that are still in place today have seven heads, rather than nine. Moreover, the five gateways in the city walls are all surmounted by four heads rather than five. So did Zhou make a mistake? We know that the stonework of the city was reworked by successive kings, so perhaps Zhou did see nine *naga* and five faces, with the stonework being modified later. Images with five heads or faces were certainly not unknown at the time; there are examples in the National Museum in Phnom Penh. See also figures 5 and 6.

11. The trees on the walls, which Zhou calls *guanglang* 桄榔, are likely to be *arenga pinnata*, sugar palm, which is what *guanglang* means today. Other sources identify *guanglang* with sago palm. CH, 3392; E. Chan, *Forest Plants of Indonesia* (Singapore: Periplus, 1998), 25; xn, 51.

The insides of the walls are still heavily banked with sloping earth and stone, forming a broad rampart. The phrase "… over a hundred feet in width" is in Zhou's words "perhaps some ten *zhang* 丈 " or some 103 feet. The description of a slope with gates on it is hard to visualize, and perhaps the text here is corrupt. A sentence here about criminals is certainly out of place in the original text, and I have moved it down to go with the sentence about dogs.

Although Zhou refers to sides rather than corners, his mention of the towers on the four sides of the wall may refer to the temples dedicated to Lokesvara at the corners or sub-cardinal points of the wall, each of which has a small tower.

Here as later Zhou uses the term *ta* 塔 for tower. For him *ta* would have meant both tower and Buddhist stupa, which in China often took the form of a pagoda. I have translated *ta* as tower, pagoda, or stupa, depending on context.

12. Assuming the gold tower is the Bayon, there is now a stone terrace rather than a bridge on the east side. The gold Buddhas have gone, but the terrace is still guarded by two lions, now just made of plain stone. The Bayon is thought to have had fifty-four towers, though by a recent count there are now only thirty-seven. Zhou's figure of twenty or so may correspond to the main towers in the inner part of the building.

Zhou writes that the Bayon was at "the center of the state (*guo*)." Again, I have taken *guo* here to mean primarily "the capital city" of the state.

Since he gives no recognizable names, the places Zhou mentions in this chapter—Bayon, Bapuon, Phimeanakas, Bakheng, Angkor Wat, East Mebon, and Neak Pean—are identified mainly from his description of their location and design. XN, 54–64; PP, 134–144.

Zhou refers here and later to gold towers, gold Buddhas, a bronze elephant, and so on. It is not clear what he means by describing things as gold or bronze. Whatever the case, larger objects were presumably painted, covered with gilded stucco (traces of which survive in Angkor Wat), or plated with gold or bronze, rather than being entirely made of these materials. Zhou himself alludes to some form of covering when he writes in this chapter of the heads over the gateways being "decorated with gold." A temple inscription about "houses . . . ornamented with shining gold" gives the same impression. Many of the structures and sculptures that Zhou mentions as being of gold or bronze are still extant, but are now objects made of plain stone, suggesting that the gold, bronze, gold stucco, and paintwork that once covered them has been taken or just lost through erosion. Chandler, *A History of Cambodia*, 41; M. Freeman and C. Jacques, *Ancient Angkor* (Bangkok: River Books, 2003), 29.

13. This tower is evidently Bapuon, though Bapuon lies northwest of Bayon rather than north of it. Currently the subject of a massive restoration effort, the

semi-collapsed state of Bapuon precludes much useful comparison between the present state of the structure and what Zhou describes. There is an earlier description in *Treatise on the Various Foreigners*, later alluded to in the brief *Song shi* (*History of the Song Dynasty*) account of Cambodia, of a bronze terrace "in the southwest corner" of the royal palace "that has twenty-four bronze towers guarded by eight bronze elephants" each weighing over two tons. This seems to be a description of Bapuon too. (The bronze elephants "each weighed four thousand *jin* 斤," *jin* being units of weight equivalent to about 633 grams or 22 ounces avoirdupois, meaning that each elephant weighed 2.5 metric tons or 2.8 US tons. The word used to describe the elephants, *tong* 銅, seems to have meant bronze (*qing tong* 青銅) rather than copper; this is also true of *tong* as used by Zhou, except in chapters 21 and 30, where he seems to be describing copper utensils).

14. The king's residence is the Royal Palace, so the gold tower must be Phimeanakas, site of the king's nightly liaison with a serpent spirit as described in chapter 2. Today Phimeanakas is the main structure still standing in the compound of the royal palace, which was made mostly of wood that later decayed, apart from two stone-rimmed ponds or tanks, a stone-lined pit, and a surrounding wall with gates.

Here and elsewhere Zhou uses the term *guozhu* 國主, "head of state" or "sovereign," for king. In his text the usual Chinese term for king (*wang* 王) is only used three times, twice in chapter 2 in references to the "foreign king" (*fan wang* 番王) of Cambodia and once in chapter 35 in a textual variant for the king of Champa. Given the intermittent relations between Cambodia and the Yuan court, his avoidance of the term "king" may have been out of concern for protocol. Similarly he refers to the king's palace as *guogong* 國宮, "state palace," or in other more indirect ways (*chu* 處, *hu* 戶, *nei* 內). I have used the terms king and royal palace, since more literal translations read awkwardly or have the wrong connotations.

15. "...noble Cambodia": here Zhenla in original. Stone Tower Mountain seems to be Phnom Bakheng, the seventy-five-meter hill surmounted by the Bakheng temple where tourists now gather daily to see the sunset.

"Lu Ban's tomb" evidently refers to Angkor Wat. This is Zhou's only—very brief—reference to this structure, completed more than a century before his visit. It is astonishing that he says so little about so dramatic a site, while being so impressed by other less extraordinary places such as Bapuon. Perhaps for some reason he did not see Angkor Wat with his own eyes; or perhaps he wrote more extensively about it but what he wrote was later lost.

The reference to Lu Ban is puzzling. In Chinese history or mythology Lu Ban was a carpenter from Confucius' state of Lu in northern China who lived sometime between the eighth and the fifth century BCE. Lu Ban's involvement in the civilization of Angkor was inconceivable, both culturally and chronologically. One explanation for Zhou's otherwise bizarre references to him is that by Zhou's time he had already acquired mythical, godlike qualities, and that Zhou or others—Zhou's local Chinese guides perhaps—confused Lu Ban with another god, Visvakarman, the Hindu god of carpenters. According to this explanation, Zhou took Lu Ban to be the same as Visvakarman, and then mistook Visvakarman for Suryavarman II, the king who had Angkor Wat built, perhaps as his own mausoleum. The two individuals could have been confused quite easily because Visvakarman was popularly known in Cambodia as Brah Bisnukar. This name was almost the same as Brah Bisnulok, the popular form of Suryavarman II's posthumous title, Parama-Visnuloka. This explanation was put forward by Louis Finot as part of an essay, "The Temple of Angkor Wat," first published in 1929. It is reproduced in an English translation in Smithies, tr. and ed., *The Customs of Cambodia*, 128–129.

The fact that Zhou refers to Angkor Wat as a tomb gives weight to the view that it was indeed built as a mausoleum.

16. The East Lake is the East Baray, at the center of which is East Mebon temple. There is nothing to suggest that the temple housed a reclining Buddha. On the other hand, part of a gigantic reclining Vishnu made in bronze (now in the National Museum in Phnom Penh) was recovered with the help of a local farmer by the French archaeologist Maurice Glaize on the other side of Angkor Thom, near the temple called West Mebon in the West Baray. It has been

suggested that this is what Zhou was referring to, though there are no textual variants to support the theory. Freeman and Jacques, *Ancient Angkor*, 188; M. Glaize, *Les Monuments du Groupe d'Angkor* (Paris: J. Maisonneuve, 2003), 270.

There is another sentence in the text at this point that is found only in the later work *Cheng zhai za ji* (*Cheng Zhai's Miscellany* 誠齋雜記). It reads that the water spouting from the reclining Buddha "tastes like Chinese wine, and quickly makes people drunk." The *Miscellany* may have quoted from a version of Zhou's text that was later changed or lost, though this is conjecture. PP. 55–61.

17. The square—actually, cruciform—gold tower is Neak Pean, built in the last part of the twelfth century, during the reign of Jayavarman VII. Neak Pean is in the middle of the man-made lake called Jayatataka Baray, to the north of Angkor Thom. As the site is now, it consists of a tower in the middle of a pond, which is linked to smaller ponds by four small chapels. In all four chapels there are stone images with mouths that serve as water-spouts. They include images of an elephant, a lion, and a horse—just as Zhou says. The site evidently represents the sacred Himalayan lake of Anavatapta, famous as the source of four great rivers issuing north, south, east, and west from the mouths of a lion, an elephant, an ox, and a horse, respectively. For some reason the elephant and the lion in Neak Pean are in the wrong places, being in the north and south chapels respectively, and where there should be an ox in the east chapel there is the head of a man.

Among the many descriptions of Anavatapta there is a good one in the Chinese account of the Chinese monk Xuanzang's journey to India in the seventh century CE (which I mentioned in the introduction as being comparable to Zhou's memoirs, but much longer). The description reads:

> In the middle of the Land of Jambu is Lake Anavatapta, to the south of the Fragrant Mountains and to the north of the Great Snowy Mountains. It is eight hundred *li* in circumference. Its banks are decorated with gold, silver, lapis lazuli, and glass crystals. Golden sand stretches far and wide,

and its clear waters are bright and smooth as a mirror. Through the power of his will a Bodhisattva changed himself into a snake and lives hidden in the middle of the lake, putting forth clear, cool water for the Land of Jambu. By this means the waters of the River Ganges flow from the mouth of a silver ox on the east side of the lake, encircle the lake once, and go into the Southeastern Sea. The waters of the Sindhu flow from the mouth of a gold elephant on the south side of the lake, encircle the lake once, and go into the Southwestern Sea. The waters of the Oxus flow out of the mouth of a lapis lazuli horse on the west side of the lake, encircle the lake once, and go into the Northwestern Sea. And the waters of the Yarkand flow out of the mouth of a glass crystal lion on the north side of the lake, circle the lake once, and go into the Northeastern Sea. (*Da tang xi yu ji* 大唐西域記, *Great Tang Dynasty Record of the Western Regions* (Beijing: Zhonghua shuju, 1985), 39 (my translation).)

Most of the lengths and distances Zhou gives in this chapter are fairly rough and ready, and only a few of them correspond to actual lengths and distances, assuming that a *li* was half a kilometre and three *zhang* were equal to slightly less than 10 meters. For example, the city walls are actually about 12 kilometers or 7½ miles in circumference, rather than the 10 kilometers or 7 miles (20 *li*) that Zhou estimates. The walls are about 8 meters or 26 feet high, rather than 6.3 meters or 21 feet (2 *zhang*) as Zhou supposes. The inner slopes or ramparts are hard to measure but Zhou's estimate of some 31 meters or 103 feet (10 *zhang*) seems too large. Bapuon is 200 meters north of Bayon, rather than half a kilometer (1 *li*). The distance from Bapuon to the royal palace is less than Zhou's estimate of half a kilometer (1 *li*)—the outermost enclosure of Bapuon actually borders the royal palace to the north—though the distance between the two depends on whether it is measured from perimeter to perimeter or central point to central point. Phnom Bakheng is 400 meters from the south gate, rather than 250 meters (half a *li*). Angkor Wat is 1.7 kilometers or a mile south of Angkor Thom, rather than a third of that distance (1 *li*).

By contrast, Zhou's figure for the circumference of Angkor Wat is quite accurate, and suggests he was given fairly precise measurements. It is 5.6 kilometers or 3½ miles in circumference, not very different from Zhou's figure of 10 *li*. Zhou seems to have overestimated the size of the East Lake, which is about 18 kilometers or 11 miles in circumference rather than 50 kilometers or 33 miles (100 *li*). The same applies even if he is referring to the West Lake rather than the East Lake, since the two lakes are not very different in size. On the other hand his estimate of the distance of the lake from the city is accurate, if the distance considered is from the center of the lake to the city wall, which is about 5 kilometers or 3 miles (10 *li*). Likewise his estimate of the distance of the North Lake from the city is accurate if measured from the center of the lake to the city wall—about 2½ kilometers or 1.7 miles (5 *li*). On the distances as measured today, see Freeman and Jacques, *Ancient Angkor*, 47, 103; D. Rooney, *Angkor: An Introduction to the Temples* (New York: W. W. Norton, 2004), 147, 149, 159, 214, 234; *Cambodia Country Map* (Singapore: Periplus Editions, ? 2004).

Chapter 2: Residences

18. The gold tower is again evidently the Bayon. Depending on what Zhou is referring to as the palace, he overestimates its size. Five to six *li* equal 2½ to 3 kilometers or 1.7 to 2 miles. The circumference of the laterite wall around the palace is in fact just under 1.7 kilometers, or just over a mile. But perhaps Zhou was including other areas as well, for example the open area east of the palace, including the Leper King Terrace. Freeman and Jacques, *Ancient Angkor*, 111.

19. The tower is Phimeanakas. The "foreign king" Zhou refers to is, of course, the Cambodian king. "... at the summit of which" is a variant reading. Other texts have "at the base of which." For *xia* 下 read *shang* 上 as in the Ming *Shuo fu*. The structure of Phimeanakas is such that the chamber at the top of it would have been more suitable for the tryst.

Chapter 3: Dress

20. The Chinese phrase *zhui ji* 椎髻 suggests hair bound up into a tall knot or bun resembling a club or cudgel, which is what *zhui* 椎 means. The phrase was in use as early as Han dynasty times, CH, 3444. Reliefs at Bayon and Angkor Wat show a variety of hairstyles, including frequently a small, neat bun or topknot. See figure 15.

The term used for cloth, *bu* 布, does not specify what it is made from. "Ounce," or Chinese ounce, is the English equivalent of *liang* 兩, which was also formerly known in English as tael. There were sixteen Chinese ounces or taels in a catty or *jin*, and the weight of a *jin* was 633 grams or 22 ounces avoirdupois (note 13). Zhou writes that the pearl around the king's neck weighed about three *jin*.

No one is sure which places "Western Seas" refers to. Parts of India made a good living from their trade in cotton and other cloth, as we know from Marco Polo, so somewhere in India seems likely. But Zhou (or the Cambodians) may have had other locations in mind, including the Malayan peninsula.

21. The text in Chinese reads: "like what is worn on the head of the *vajra* (*jingang* 金剛)." *Jingang* or *vajra* means "diamond" in the Buddhist sense of the term. Here it seems to mean *jingang chi* 金剛持, or in Sanskrit *vajradhara*, Holder of the Diamond. The Holder of the Diamond is the Buddha, sometimes called the Primordial Buddha, who is most often associated with Vajrayana or Diamond Vehicle beliefs. (Another deity associated with the Diamond Vehicle and known to have been worshipped in Cambodia in the thirteenth century is Hevajra.) The tantric beliefs of the Diamond Vehicle were widespread in east Asia in the thirteenth century, and later became a central influence in China during the Manchu period. By comparing king Indravarman III to the Holder of the Diamond, Zhou seems to be suggesting that tantric Buddhism was an important part of the king's worldview. This stands in contrast to the fact that, as noted in the introduction, Theravada Buddhism was increasingly influential in Cambodia at the time. Ren J., ed., *Fojiao da cidian* (Shanghai: Jiangsu guji chubanshe, 2002), 788, 796; K. Trainor, *Buddhism: The Illustrated Guide* (New York: Oxford University Press, 2001), 162–165.

22. Cat's eye gemstones are a variety of chrysoberyl that have a distinct band of light across them that moves from side to side when they are moved.

The golden sword the king carries appears to have had ritual significance as a symbol of the state. In the last chapter the king is again described as carrying it as if it were a kind of emblem of office.

Anding basha 暗丁八殺 [P *amting pasa*] seems to mean something like "not knowing the customs." *Basha* seems to be the Cambodian word for language (*pee-a-saa*), itself from the Sanskrit *bhasa*, from which the sense of "customs" seems to have been derived. *Anding* has not been clearly identified and may be a textual corruption, though as David Chandler has suggested (personal communication) it is tempting to identify *ding* with the Khmer *deung*, "know, understand," even though *jeh* rather than *deung* is the word now used in Khmer when talking about knowing a language. *Anding* occurs with apparently quite different meanings in this and the following chapter, suggesting that in one or other place it has erroneously replaced another word or phrase. PP, 64–65, LRP 25, 80, 27, 273.

Here Zhou makes his first reference to locally based Chinese. The term for Chinese people that Zhou uses throughout is *Tang ren* 唐人, people of the Tang, the term still used today in the Chinese expression for Chinatowns in England and America, *Tang ren jie* 唐人街, "Streets of the people of Tang." The term *Tang ren* was widely used from the Song dynasty onward. As *Ming shi* puts it: "Foreigners all call Chinese people 'people of the Tang.' It is the same in all the countries overseas." *Ming shi, juan* 324, 8395; XN, 90.

Chapter 4: Officials

23. The word *yi* 亦, normally meaning "also," appears twice in this paragraph. As Pelliot suggests, in the first instance (though not in the second instance, when it does mean "also") the sense of the word may be "as in China," which is how the term is translated here at the beginning of the paragraph. This sense of the term seems to occur elsewhere in the text, too.

The point of Zhou's comment about concubines is not entirely clear. He seems to be saying that by giving the king a concubine, office-holders who are not his relatives are compensating for that fact.

24. In South Asia the palanquin or palankin—a bed or a place to sit or lie on, hung from a pole and carried by two or more people—goes back to the days of the Indian classic epic *Ramayana*. In its fourteen-century Indian form the Moroccan traveler Ibn Battuta described it as being "like a bed of state ... with a pole of wood above ... this is curved, and made of the Indian cane, solid and compact. Eight men, divided into two relays, are employed in turn to carry one of these; four carry the palankin while four rest." The English word palanquin probably comes from the Sanskrit *palyanka*, a bed, via Indian languages and Portuguese. In Cambodia, friezes on the Bayon and at Angkor Wat suggest that palanquins were very much part of daily life. They are shown bearing women and holy men, and came in more than one shape, a common one being with a pole that was vertical at both ends and arched in the middle. Zhou describes Cambodian palanquins in more detail in chapter 31. In China the palanquin, *jiao* 較, also has a long history, dating back two millennia. Officials regarded it as especially useful for crossing mountain passes. The celebrated twelfth-century Chinese poet Yang Wanli 楊萬里 wrote in a poem about crossing mountains that he was worried about his palanquin "eating into the shoulders of the carriers." Ibn Battuta is quoted from HJ, 659; Yang Wanli is in CH, 3523.

25. The terms for which *anding* 暗丁, *bading* 巴丁, and *siladi* 廝辣的 are transliterations have not been identified. As noted above (note 22), the recurrence of *anding* here, so soon after its use with another meaning in chapter 3, suggests a corruption of the text in one place or the other. For further discussion on titles that may be relevant, PP, 65; XN, 93; Vickery, *Society, Economics and Politics in Pre-Angkor Cambodia*, 190 and following, 433–435.

I have added the words "except for" to make better sense of the last sentence.

Chapter 5: The Three Doctrines

26. The three Khmer words here probably mean pundit, Buddhist monk, and Saivite or worshipper of the god Shiva. The first, *banjie* 班詰, [P *pankhi*, K *pwank'iet*] seems to derive from the Sanskrit *pandita* (though the aspirated *k* sound in *pwank'iet* is incongruous), meaning pundit or learned man. The second, *zhugu* 苧姑, seems to be derived from *chaokhun* (*kh* here represents the aspirated *k*, following the conventional system for transliterating Thai), the respectful title used for Theravada Buddhist monks in Siam. As for *basiwei* 八思惟, Georges Coedès argues that it is a transcription of the last two syllables of the Sanskrit word *tapasvi*, meaning ascetic. He notes that there are inscriptions at Angkor referring to *tapasvi*, one of them identifying them as Sivaites or Saivites, that is, worshippers of Siva. Saivites are lingam-worshippers, and Zhou's description of *basiwei* as stone-worshippers also suggests they were Saivites, or at least had some affinity with them. G. Coedès, "Nouvelles Notes sur Tcheou Ta-kouan," *T'oung Pao*, series 2, vol. 30 (1933), 224–225; PP, 65; XN, 96; LRP, 28, 154; GSP, 69, 111.

In a striking instance of his Chinese worldview, Zhou describes these three types of religious devotees in terms of the three orthodox doctrines of China, Confucianism, Buddhism, and Daoism. Zhou calls pundits *ru zhe* 儒者, scholars in the Confucian tradition, though they were clearly Hindu rather than Confucian. Likewise he calls the *basiwei* "Daoist," although as Saivites (assuming that was what they were) their antecedents were again Hindu rather than Chinese Daoist. The only one of the three doctrines that China and Cambodia shared in a broad sense was Buddhism.

27. Sakyamuni, one of the Buddha's commonest epithets, means "Sage of the Sakyas" and refers to the fact that he was from the Sakya clan. *Bolai* 孛賴 [P *polaj*, K *b'uetlai*] may be the word *prah*, a word used in one form or another for the Buddha in Cambodia, Siam, and Burma. LRP, 40, 181; GSR, 134, 86.

28. The leaves of the fan-palm or palmyra—palmyra being a Portuguese word meaning palm-tree—have been used to write on since the fifth century AD. Buddhist sutras brought to China from India were written on them,

making them greatly treasured, so much so that during the Tang dynasty a palmyra was planted in the Chinese capital Chang'an. To make the material for a manuscript the leaves are cut into rectangular strips and threaded together in a form recognizable to anyone who has been to a Cambodian market.

29. In contrast, Zhou would have meant, to China.

30. The word Zhou uses for "tall headdress" is *gugu* 罟姑, the Chinese term (also written with various other characters) for a particular form of Mongolian headdress, a tall, hollow structure sometimes reinforced with wire. It seems quite like the one described by the thirteenth-century Flemish monk William of Rubruck in his account of the Mongol court at Khara Khorum in central Asia. William wrote that the women "have a head-dress ... made of bark, or such other light material as they can find, and it is big and as much as two hands can span around, and is a cubit and more high, and square like the capital of a column. This ... they cover with costly silk stuff, and it is hollow inside, and on top of the capital, or the square on it, they put a tuft of quills or light canes also a cubit or more in length." Zhou specifically refers to Tartars rather than Mongols, but he may be using the term loosely to indicate Mongols in general, rather than referring specifically to the Tatar tribe of the eastern steppes. On William of Rubruck, www.gotheborg.com/glossary. On Tatars and Tartars, Mote, *Imperial China*, 409.

31. The stone blocks are reminiscent of the stone lingams worshipped by Saivites, while the comparison with Chinese gods of the earth suggests that like some Western scholars Zhou perceives a connection between the stones and local spirit worship.

Chapter 6: The People

32. The meaning of the first part of the text is in dispute, and the text may be corrupt. One interpretation is: "The local people only know the customs of the southern barbarians. They are coarse and ugly, and very black. This is not only the case of those who live ... ," taking *ren* 人 to mean the local people rather than people in general, and *zhi* 知 in the phrase *shu buzhi* 殊不知 to be an error for

zhi 只 "only." By contrast I have accepted Xia Nai's punctuation, which treats the first twelve characters as a single sentence reading: "People only know that people with southern barbarian customs are coarse, ugly, and very black." PP, 15; Smithies, *The Customs of Cambodia*, 15; XN, 101.

For southern barbarians Zhou uses the disparaging term *man* 蠻. It is a term the Chinese applied to various unassimilated peoples of southern China, Annam (present-day northern Vietnam), and beyond. The character *man* is still used today in the Chinese term *yeman* 野蠻, "uncivilized, savage." On barbarians being seen to be black: F. Dikötter, *The Discourse of Race in Modern China* (London: Hurst & Co., 1992), 7–18. Perhaps people in China knew the Cambodians were "ugly and black" because it was a description dating back to Funan times: Briggs, *The Ancient Khmer Empire*, 29; also page 132 below.

Nanpeng 南棚, "southern canopy," may be a transliteration of a Khmer word, but if so it is not clear which one. The gloss in the text explaining *nanpeng* is in the original.

Given the mildly sensuous adjective he uses (*su* 酥, "smooth like milk or butter"), Zhou has been taken to be writing mainly about the milky-white breasts of women when he writes about the top parts of bodies being uncovered. However his text refers to men and women with equal emphasis, and uses a term for chest, *xiong* 胸, that like older usages of the English word breast applies equally well to both sexes. Moreover *su* describes smoothness of texture rather than color.

33. "... one principal wife": The text actually has "one for the main room (*zheng shi* 正室)." This is a common phrase for "first wife," but in this context suggests that the king's sleeping quarters may actually have been constructed with a central room and rooms on each side of it pointing north, south, east, and west.

34. *Chenjialan* 陳家蘭 [P *tshinkjalan*, K *d'ienkalan*] has not been satisfactorily explained. It has been identified with several possible words in Cambodian and Sanskrit, including the Sanskrit *srngara*, meaning adornment, sexual passion. XN, 103; LRP, 52, 143, 182; GSR, 107, 28, 69.

The northerners are evidently northern Chinese. I have not found any other reference to the particular hairstyle Zhou refers to, called literally "open waterway" (*kai shui dao* 開水道), and have guessed at some form of shaved parting.

Vermilion is the bright red pigment made by grinding down red sulphide of mercury, or cinnabar. Its bright red color was—and is—favored as the color of blood, life, and eternity. Cinnabar was treasured by Chinese Daoists, since it could be changed easily into quicksilver and offered a startling example of the transmutation of things. Cinnabar thus came to be seen as the likely source of an elixir of eternal life. The Chinese search for an elixir using cinnabar started in the fourth century CE and went on for over a millennium. By the time of the Tang dynasty many Chinese recognized that while good cinnabar came from China it also came from beyond China's borders in the deep south. E. Schafer, *The Vermilion Bird* (Berkeley and Los Angeles: University of California Press, 1967), 157; J. Needham, *Science and Civilization in China, Volume 3: Mathematics and the Sciences of the Heavens and Earth* (Cambridge: Cambridge University Press, 1959), 87 and following.

35. *Er xing ren* 二形人 has been taken to refer to gay men, but means literally "people with two forms or appearances" and could describe epicene or transgender qualities rather than homosexuality as such. *Er xing ren* is gender-neutral but probably refers to men.

Chapter 7: Childbirth

36. "... the local women": Zhou uses the term *fan*, foreign, referring to *fan nu* 番女, foreign women. From here on I use "local" for *fan*.

The term *shoulian* 收斂 has a medical meaning, "contract," that suggests that it is the physical condition of the vagina that reverts to that of a young girl.

37. Zhu Maichen 朱買臣 was a Chinese official in the second century BCE who was abandoned by his wife. The full story or homily as related in *Han shu* 漢書, the official history of the Former Han dynasty, is that when Zhu Maichen was

poor his wife left him; he then became a high official, and she so regretted what she had done that she committed suicide. XN, 105–106.

Chapter 8: Young Girls

38. *Zhentan* 陣毯 [P *tsintham*] is probably from a Khmer word, but if so the word has not been identified. The ritual described in this chapter is also described in another Yuan dynasty compendium of Chinese travel writings, *Yi yu ji* 異域志, *Treatise on Strange Frontier Lands*, by Zhou Zhizhong. XN, part 3, 24. LRP, 402, 301.

The explanation that the month is the fourth in the Chinese calendar is Zhou's. He is telling his Chinese readers which month it is by their reckoning, not saying that the Cambodians consciously used a Chinese calendar.

39. As made clear in chapter 5, the people Zhou calls Daoists were probably Saivaites.

"... the poor do not have the leisure to choose": *yi* 亦 is omitted as in the *Si ku quan shu* 四庫全書 variant. XN, 106.

The word picul, used here for the Chinese word *dan* 擔, is now archaic, having been used in China in European colonial times. I have used it here partly because the more modern equivalent in tons reads so incongruously. In Yuan times one *dan* generally consisted of a hundred *jin*, that is, about 137 pounds or 63 kilos. A hundred piculs would thus have been some 6.3 metric tons or nearly 7 US tons—an inconceivably large amount. Something seems wrong, either with the presumed size of the Yuan dynasty picul or *dan*, or with the text. All we can reliably take from this passage is that the largest donations were very large indeed. (Thanks to David Chandler for making the point that ton equivalents would read confusingly.)

Betel nuts come from the betel nut or areca palm tree *binlang* 檳榔 and are wrapped in the leaves of the betel vine to make the digestive quid for chewing so widely enjoyed in South Asia. They were long regarded as a delicacy in China, as in Cambodia, and in Tang times Chinese hosts gave them to guests as a special treat. Schafer, *The Vermilion Bird*, 175.

40. That is, the night of 29–30 April 1297.

Chapter 9: Slaves

41. The term Zhou uses for savages, *ye ren* 野人, literally means "wild or uncivilized people." His attitude, typical of the time, is reflected in the fact that he uses a term to signify slaves that is more usually used for small objects than for human beings. Later the terms he uses for male and female slaves are those used for animals.

Who were the Zhuang 撞 of Cambodia? Opinions differ as to their identity, but there is no particular reason to suppose that they were related to the Zhuang 壯 nationality in Southwest China, despite the similarity between an old character 僮 used for the Zhuang of China and the one Zhou uses for the Cambodian Zhuang.

42. Cambodian houses were built on stilts then, as today.

43. *Batuo* 巴駝 cannot be identified as a Cambodian word, though it seems similar to a Cham word for king. *Mi* 米 [P *mi*, K *miei*] is close to *mai*, "mother" in Khmer. pp, 63–65; lrp, 213; gsr, 160.

44. The text is not explicit about the form of the shackles. The arm and leg shackles may have joined an individual slave's arms or legs together by means of a shackle or iron clasp on each limb and a chain linking the clasps—but this is just a guess.

Chapter 10: Language

45. The transliterations are transliterations of the numbers from one to ten in Khmer, the numbers being *moo-ay, bpee, bay, boo-un, bprum, bprum moo-ay, bprum bpee, bprum bay, bprum boo-un, dop.*

46. Again, these are transliterations of the Khmer words concerned. *Bang* 邦 and *buwen* 補溫 are straight forward—elder brother is *borng* in Cambodian, and younger brother is *bpaoan. Jilai* 吃賴 [P *kilaj*, K *kietlai*] is less straightforward, but may represent *t'lai*, the Cambodian word for brother-in-law. pp, 69; lrp, 139, 181; gsr, 141, 86. The pronunciation of 吃 as *ji* not *chi* follows Pulleyblank.

47. Zhang San 張三 means "Zhang the Third" and Li Si 李四 means "Li the Fourth"—informal names indicating that their owners are the third- and fourth-

born in their families. This is still a common Chinese practice today, similar to the old British practice of addressing the two sons of a family called Jones as Jones Major and Jones Minor.

48. Of the three Cambodian words Zhou uses here, two were introduced earlier (*bading* in chapter 4, and *banjie* in chapter 5). The third, *Beishi* 備世 [P *Pujsi*, K *B'jisiäi*], is new, and its meaning and origins are in doubt. There is no record elsewhere of a word resembling Beishi being used as a name for China. Its Tang pronunciation B'jisiäi has some affinity with the word Vijaya—a word associated variously with Srivijaya in Sumatra and the Philippines (Visaya). But neither of these associations seems suitable here. One alternative, Coedès suggests, is that *b'jisiäi* is the Sanskrit word *visaya*, realm or kingdom, used here as a respectful metonym for China. PP, 66; Coedès, "Nouvelles Notes sur Tcheou Takouan," 225–226; LRP, 31, 285; GSR, 259, 99. Pulleyblank's reconstruction of the Yuan sound, Pujsi, may put this explanation in doubt; but then again, the word may have been an old one.

The word Zhou uses here for "scholars," and only here, is *xiucai* 秀才.

Chapter 11: Savages

49. "Herbal concoctions" is an elaboration of *yue* 藥 medicine, often medicine with a herbal base.

The word used for group here, *dang* 黨, is sometimes used for what we would call today a kinship group.

50. Cardamom or *dou kou* 荳蔲, valued for its fragrance and its medicinal qualities, may have originated in South India but was also found throughout Southeast Asia and in South China. The reference here seems to be to *amomum kravanh*, the cardamom found in Cambodia. The Chinese valued cardamom for its fragrance and particularly for its medicinal value—it was seen as being good for acidity and hangovers.

Kapok, often called *mumianhua* 木綿花, as Zhou calls it here, is the fine cotton-like material surrounding the seeds of certain tropical trees, including *bombax malabaricum*, also known as the silk cotton tree, and *ceiba pentandra*. *Ceiba pentandra* are among the huge trees still growing today out of the walls of the Ta Prohm temple in Angkor, left there to show the devastating effect on the Angkor temples of unchecked forest growth.

Chapter 12: Writing

51. Muntjaks or barking deer are a small Southeast Asian deer; the male has tusks and small antlers.

52. *Suo*: there is a similar word for chalk in Thai.

53. The Uighurs, now the main nationality in Xinjiang in the far west of China, were important advisers to the Mongols in China in the thirteenth century. There is no known connection between Uighur and Khmer scripts, nor indeed between the two languages. The same applies to Mongolian and Khmer.

The script used by the Uighurs in Zhou's time was based on the old Turkic alphabet. The script used by the Khmers was ultimately derived from the ancient Indian Brahmi script. This Brahmi script was written horizontally from left to right, hence the Cambodian practice of doing the same. (Zhou called it writing "from back to front," since the Chinese wrote from right to left and top to bottom.) As for the languages, the Uighurs are a Turkic-speaking people, while Mongolian belongs to the Altaic family of languages. The Khmer language, on the other hand, is one of the Mon-Khmer languages of Southeast Asia. On the Uighurs as an important source of support for the Mongols, see T. Allsen, "The Rise of the Mongolian Empire and Mongolian Rule in North China," in CHC, 349–350. On Khmer writing systems and languages: www. anu.edu.au/~u9907217languages/languages.html and www.ancientscripts. com/khmer.html

54. Who was Esen Khaya (*Yexian Haiya* 也先海牙)? Was he perhaps the head of the delegation Zhou accompanied to Cambodia? The reference to him here is certainly familiar, and the fact that he could compare Khmer and Mongolian suggests firsthand experience of both. Esen Khaya is not among those with biographies in *Yuan shi*; but two people with the name Esen Khaya are listed in the repertory of Yuan names compiled by the authority on Yuan names Igor

de Rachewiltz. The first was a *darughachi* or "resident commissioner" or local chief administrator for the Mongols, the other a middle-ranking Uighur official. Without further research it is hard to be sure whether either of these men was ever an envoy to Southeast Asia. Information from I. de Rachewiltz and M. Wang, *Repertory of Proper Names in Yüan Literary Sources* (Taipei: Southern Materials Center, 1988), vol. 3, 2289, 2700, vol. 4, 778; also personal communications from Igor de Rachewiltz. One other possibility is that Esen Khaya was related to one of the two military officers Khubilai Khan sent south into Annam in 1286–1287 following the death of General Sodu. Intriguingly the names of these two officers were Esen Temür and Arigh Khaya. See Rossabi, *Khubilai Khan: His Life and Times*, 218.

55. One textual variant has it that there are indeed such shops. xn, 119.

Chapter 13: New Year and other Times of Year

56. *Jiade* 佳得 [p *Kjatej*, k *Kaitek*] is evidently a transliteration of Karttika, the Hindu lunar month which starts in late October by the Gregorian calendar. The second day of Karttika marks the end of the festival of Divali, so called from the Sanskrit for "row of lights." Perhaps there is a connection between the lights of Divali and the lanterns and fireworks Zhou describes. lrp, 143, 74; gsr, 234, 240.

57. "A large stage is set up": The term *peng* 棚, which I have translated here as "stage," also occurs in chapter 8, where it is used in its usual sense of a canopy, or the framework for a canopy. Here the meaning seems closer to the sense of a covered framework or stage, as the comparison to scaffolding suggests. The Chinese for the phrase "scaffolding used to make a pagoda" (*zao ta pu gan*, 造塔撲竿) is open to different interpretations. I have used *ta* 塔 rather than the Ming *Shuo fu* variant *da* 搭, and taken *pu* 撲 to mean stick or pole. *Ta* here may be read as pagoda rather than tower, assuming Zhou is referring to construction work seen at home in China. xn, 136–137.

58. The firework display must have been done either inside the palace walls, or in front of the Elephant and Leper King terraces just to the east of the palace.

Zhou gives the distance of the bank or raised place (*an* 岸) from the palace as 20–30 *zhang* (around 63–95 meters, or 207–310 feet), and the height of the firework towers as 20 *zhang* or so (around 63 meters or 207 feet). A distance of 20 to 30 *zhang* from the palace would put the bank within the palace walls, somewhere near the large pond or tank on the northeast side of the palace compound. The pond is still extant, as are its finely decorated stone walls, thought to have been built by Jayavarman VIII, the king whose reign ended shortly before Zhou's visit. Otherwise the bank Zhou mentions could be the same as the one mentioned in chapter 14, in which case it would be somewhere in the area immediately outside the eastern entrance to the royal palace, near the Elephant and Leper King terraces (see also note 64).

59. The word I have translated as "the rocks thrown by trebuchets," *pao* 砲, was used in Zhou's time to describe either a trebuchet, a military engine for throwing rocks, or the actual rocks thrown from it. Later *pao* evolved into a rock-propelling engine fired by gunpowder, and later still a cannon in the Western sense of the term (the sense *pao* has in Chinese today). Weapons identifiable as cannons began to be used in China in the twelfth century CE, but Zhou probably did not have such things in mind here. Even without gunpowder, trebuchets in Zhou's time were evidently very noisy. Their missiles apparently made an immense smashing sound on impact, one that "shook heaven and earth," as a contemporary observer remarked when describing the trebuchets used by Khubilai Khan's forces in their attacks on cities in South China. See J. Needham, *Science and Civilization in China, Volume V, 7: Chemistry and Chemical Technology, Part 7* (Cambridge: Cambridge University Press, 1976), 276–284; A. Moule, *Quinsai, with Other Notes on Marco Polo* (Cambridge, 1957), quoted in CHC, 433.

60. *ya lie* 壓獵 [P *ja lje*, K *ap liäp*]. Writing in 1938 and referring to Karlgren's reconstruction of Tang sounds, Georges Coedès identifies *ya lie* with the Khmer words *roa-up* and *ree-up*, "count" and "arrange," and suggests that *ya lie* was a kind of annual population review or census, comparable to a similar activity in Siam during the Ayutthaya dynasty founded in the following century. Pulleyblank's

sound reconstruction *ja lje* makes Coedès' explanation more questionable. Coedès, "Nouvelles Notes sur Tcheou Ta-kouan," 229; LRP, 354, 194; GSR, 164, 169.

61. *Ailan* 挨藍 [K *ailam*] may be the Khmer word *roa-um*, to dance. GSR, 609, 938.

62. "Their long and short months": in Chinese the text reads literally: "but the big and small (*da xiao* 大小) are, on the other hand, entirely different from China." I have followed Pelliot here, who takes "big and small" to refer to the long 30-day and short 29-day months of the Chinese lunar calendar. (See also note 2). "Big and small" could also refer to the other things that Zhou goes on to mention, namely the size of the night watches and the length of the day cycles.

Intercalary months are extra months added to lunar calendars to make up the 11-day difference between the lunar and solar years. The Chinese had by this time developed a system of intercalation that did not depend on the insertion of a month at a particular, fixed point in the year, hence Zhou's surprise at the Cambodian practice of intercalating the ninth month and no other.

"Like China": I have followed the Ming *Shuo fu* reading with *Zhongguo* 中國, but it is awkward here; given the *yi* 亦, which conveys the meaning "as in China," *Zhongguo* may be otiose. XN, 121.

On the divisions or watches of the night, Zhou is making the point that four watches a night is odd, given China's customary practice of having five.

The "open, shut … set up, take away" cycle is a very old 12-day cycle in use in Chinese communities in China and elsewhere. It relates to the 12 "branches" (*zhi* 支) which together with the 10 "stems" (*gan* 干) make up the 60-year cycle that is a core element of Chinese astronomy and counting systems. (The Chinese also associate each of the 12 branches with an animal, a practice also to be found in Cambodia, as Zhou notes later in the chapter.) Each of the 12 branches or days has a label or tag that describes it with a simple quality such as "open" or "shut." As far as I am aware these tags first appear in the *Huai nan zi* 淮南子, a collection of Daoist, astronomical, and other writings compiled in the second century BCE. The tags in *Huai nan zi* begin with *"jian* 建, set up" and *"chu* 除, take away," and end with *"kai* 開, open" and *"bi* 閉, shut." Zhou has the tags the other way round—his text reads *kai bi jian chu* rather than *jian chu kai bi*—but his intention is clear enough. I have made it more explicit by adding the phrase "cycle of 12 days," which is not in the original text.

For many centuries the Chinese used the 12-day cycle alongside two other day cycles, a 7-day cycle and a 10-day cycle. The 7-day cycle (or week) came into use in the Song dynasty, well before Zhou's time, though he does not seem to have known about it. As for the 10-day cycle, it derives from the long, 30-day Chinese month, and has had a long history. It persists to this day in the common Chinese expression *xun* 旬, "ten days."

On the 7-day cycle and the 5 watches of the night: J. Needham, *Science and Civilization in China, Volume 3: Mathematics and the Sciences of the Heavens and the Earth* (Cambridge: Cambridge University Press, 1959), 396 and following. On the 12-day cycle: *Huai nanzi* (Jilin, 1990), 148; H. Dubs, tr. and ed., *The History of the Former Han Dynasty* (Baltimore: Waverley Press, 1938), vol. 3, 255–257.

63. These are transliterations for the Cambodian words for horse, chicken, pig, and cow. The Khmer words are *seh* for horse (for which Zhou gives *sai* 賽), *moa-un* for chicken (Zhou's *luan* 欒), *j'rook* for pig (Zhou's *zhilu* 直盧), and *goa* for cow (Zhou's *ge* 箇). These correspond with Zhou's transliterations, though he has a superfluous *bu* 卜 before *sai*. Zhou describes the animal names with the orthodox Chinese astronomical expression (*sheng xiao* 生肖). Given his interest in the Khmer language it is odd that Zhou seems to expect the Cambodians to pronounce the animals in the cycle in a Chinese way.

Chapter 14: Settling Disputes

64. The text just says "two people" (*er ren*), and it is not clear whether these two people represent the families or are the immediate disputants. In many cases they would presumably be both.

The towers are clearly Prasat Suor Prat, the twelve towers in front of the Leper King and Elephant terraces, near the eastern entrance to the royal palace. By "bank" did Zhou actually mean the two terraces themselves? Probably not, but the text is not precise enough to be sure.

Chapter 15: Leprosy and other Illnesses

65. Some think that the king who contracted leprosy was Jayavarman VII, but David Chandler has argued that if there was a leper king it is more likely to have been Jayavarman VIII, the king who reigned from 1243 or 1270 until 1295. D. Chandler, "The Legend of the Leper King (1978)," in *Facing the Cambodian Past* (Chiang Mai: Silkworm Books, 1996), 3–14.

Chapter 16: Death

66. The text has only the generic word for hawk or eagle (*ying* 鷹), but the context here suggests the vulture (in Chinese, "bald hawk," *wu ying* 兀鷹), which seems to have been native to Cambodia and is mentioned in Khmer inscriptions. J. Jacob, "The Ecology of Angkor: Evidence from the Khmer Inscriptions," in J. Jacob, *Cambodian Linguistics, Literature and History* (London: School of Oriental and African Studies, 1993), 295.

67. In the last sentence I have taken the original reading *reng* 仍, "still," rather than the Ming *Shuo fu* variant *yi* 亦, "also." Zhou seems to be saying the practice of interring kings in towers is a long-established one that is still followed.

Chapter 17: Cultivating the Land

68. "The high water mark ... can reach some seventy to eighty feet": The text reads "7 to 8 *zhang*," around 22–25 meters or 72–83 feet.

69. That is *chi* or Chinese feet, which happen to be about the same length as English feet. Five feet would be 1.6 meters.

70. "... ten feet high"—one *zhang*. Nightsoil, or human excrement, was for many centuries a basic element of Chinese farming. Its use as fertilizer was promoted in the early years of Communist rule, but has been reduced since the agricultural reforms of the early 1980s.

Chapter 18: The Landscape

71. Zhenpu is hard to pinpoint on the map (note 2) though it must have been near present-day Vung Tau on the southeastern coast of present-day Vietnam. The river with its estuary is the Mekong, which Zhou also wrote about in the preface, though he referred to it without mentioning its name. Here he calls it "the long river" (*chang jiang* 長江), though whether as a description or a proper name is not clear. *Chang Jiang* is also the Chinese name of the Yangzi, conjuring up in his Chinese reader's mind an image of the Yangzi's own massive outlet to the sea.

72. Zhou uses almost the same expression for "old trees and tall bamboos" here as he did in the preface. This whole chapter could easily have been part of the preface.

73. The basic Chinese word for cow, *niu* 牛, can mean either cow or buffalo (the latter is called, more precisely, *shui niu* 水牛), whereas the Cambodians regard the two as quite distinct and have separate words for them (*goa*, cow and *grabay*, buffalo). Reliefs at Angkor show both, and presumably the herds could be of either.

74. Zhou's geography is impressionistic, even if he is referring to the country as a whole. The large central plain of Cambodia has mountains to the north, east, and southwest of it. But the southeast consists of flatlands stretching to the Mekong Delta and the sea.

Chapter 19: Products

75. Old Chinese records of foreign countries customarily list the exotic and valuable items available in those countries, and records of Cambodia are no different. *The Treatise on the Various Foreigners*, for example, lists a number of local Cambodian products, including elephant tusks, beeswax, kingfisher feathers

(which it notes are especially plentiful), perfumes of various kinds, raw silk, silk cloth, and sappan—the latter a kind of wood producing a red dye. It is not clear why Zhou does not mention some of Cambodia's well-known products, sappan for example. xn, 142–143.

Among the items on Zhou's list of fine things, kingfisher feathers were particularly prized as items of decoration on fashionable dresses. According to Edward Schafer, "Dresses shimmering with kingfisher feathers, fit for the gods, are virtually as old as written records in China." Schafer, *The Vermilion Bird*, 238.

All the items on Zhou's list of less refined things yield resins as well as seeds or oils for medicinal use.

Rosewood is one of the English names currently used for *jiang zhen xiang* 降真香, which previously went by such names as cayolaque and laka wood. This is not the type of rosewood used for furniture, but a reddish, mildly fragrant wood taken from the heart of a tree, *dalbergia odorifera* or a related tree, whose extract the Chinese have long valued as a medicine for stomach, blood, and other disorders. hj, 177; cmm, 428, and a number of herbal medicine websites including www.naturalmedicine.cc.

(When writing of the rosewood, Zhou refers to the Chinese inch [*cun* 寸]. There were ten *cun* in a Chinese foot [*chi* 尺], so a Chinese inch was slightly longer than a British or American inch.)

The flowers and seeds of cardamom, which Zhou mentions in chapter 11 (see note 50), were thought to have valuable medicinal qualities.

The next item *hua huang* 畫黃 is hard to identify. Pelliot suggests it is gamboge, an orange-colored medicinal resin which as its name suggests is closely associated with Cambodia. cmm identifies *teng huang* 籐黃 as gamboge. cmm, 182. An alternative textual reading, *jiang huang* 薑黃, seems to mean turmeric, which does not fit the description of *hua huang* given later in the chapter.

Lac is the resin secreted on certain trees by the lac insect and used as a varnish. It is not related to the laka wood of *jiang zhen xiang*. In Zhou's text lac is referred to by the usual Chinese name for it, *zi geng* 紫梗; the word lac comes from Sanskrit. The crude form of lac is stick lac. When it has been melted and the red dye in it has been taken away, it forms thin flakes called shellac, from which the colored varnish called lacquer is made. HJ, 499. (The mulberry mistletoe that Zhou refers to in his discussion of lac is called mulberry parasite [*sang jisheng* 桑寄生] in Chinese, and that is what it is—a parasite.)

The chaulmoogra is a tree whose seed oil was once used to treat leprosy. Its Chinese name is *da feng zi* 大風子; the English name chaulmoogra comes from its name in Bengali. CMM, 201.

If his figures are accurate, Zhou is describing a serious trading business. When writing of the beeswax, he actually says that each honeycomb weighs from 18–19 *jin* 斤 to 30–40 *jin*. Given that one *jin* was around 22 ounces or 633 grams, a trading junk carrying three thousand combs of beeswax weighing 40 *jin* each would be carrying a cargo weighing 165,000 lbs. That's nearly 76 metric tons or 84 US tons—a heavy load. Considering the size of the transaction Zhou describes, it has been suggested that he may actually have written "every year (*mei yi nian* 每一年)" rather than "every junk (*mei yi chuan* 每一船)," but there is no textual variant to support this (XN, 143).

76. Wild hops is one of the English names for *lü cao zi*, 綠草子, also known as Japanese hops. CH, 1315; CMM, 209. The *pepper Zhou* writes about is not capsicum but the spice *piper nigrum*, which grows green on the vine and turns black when picked and dried.

Chapter 21: Sought-after Chinese Goods

77. Zhou writes "the five colors," an expression that sometimes referred to what the Chinese considered to be the five main colors—dark green, vermilion, yellow, white, and black. But they also used the expression "five colors" to mean "many colors," and I have taken it to mean that here.

78. The places Zhou mentions are all cities in southeast China, most of them involved in trade with southeast Asia and further afield. Zhenzhou 真州 is up the Yangzi river from Shanghai, not far from Nanjing 南京. Wenzhou 溫州 is Zhou's home town, being the port city south of present-day Shanghai 上海 discussed in the introduction. Quanzhou 泉州 is the great port discussed in the introduction.

Chuzhou 處州, inland from Wenzhou, was the site of the Longquan 龍泉 kilns where celadon was made, and also a center for porcelain and lacquer products.

The name celadon—*qingci* 青甕 or "green pottery" in Chinese—comes from the name of the green-clad hero of a work by the now-forgotten seventeenth-century French writer Honoré d'Urfé, which happened to be vogue in Europe at the same time as *qingci* was. Archaeologists excavating the royal palace in Angkor have found remains of Chinese porcelain dating from Song, Yuan, and Ming times. XN, 149.

79. Saltpeter or potassium nitrate was used for medicine and gunpowder. Lovage, more specifically Sichuan lovage, is one of the names for *chuan qiong* 川 芎, an herb used to cure aches and pains and improve blood circulation. The text actually has *cao qiong* 草芎 rather than *chuan qiong*, but the two may be the same. XN, 150; CMM, 123. Yellow grasscloth is a literal translation of *huang cao bu* 黃草布, a material I cannot identify. The tung or *tong* 桐 tree is a tree of the genus *aleurites*, whose seed oil is good for varnishing.

The term Zhou uses for fine-toothed comb, *biji* 箆箕, seems to be a dialect word from his home town Wenzhou. XN, 150–151.

Mingzhou is the port near his home town that Zhou mentions in the general preface as the place he started from and returned to.

Mai (here translated "wheat") can mean barley (*da mai* 大麥) as well as wheat (*xiao mai* 小麥), but here it apparently means wheat, as Zhou also mentions it in chapter 28 as one of the missing ingredients that accounts for the lack of soy sauce in Cambodia. We know the emperor Chengzong tried to enforce some trade protection rules: it seems that beans and wheat were prohibited as external trade items under those rules.

Chapter 22: Flora

80. *Mei* 梅 (*prunus mume*) and *li* 李 (*prunus salicina*) are usually both translated plum, but I have translated *mei* by one of its other names, flowering apricot. The two characters *Qi zhong* 其中 "among them" before the sentence about lotus

flowers are not needed, and I have followed the Ming *Shuo fu*, which does not have them.

There does not seem to be any particular organizing principle behind Zhou's list of flora.

The last sentence as a whole seems out of place, unless it is an attempt to counter Chinese readers' complacency by ending up with something strikingly positive. I have given it that sense, though in fact the text reads simply: "there are also lotus flowers in the first month."

Chapter 23: Birds

81. A siskin is an olive-green songbird like a goldfinch.

Chapter 24: Animals

82. The chapter is entitled literally "Animals that Walk," meaning quadrupeds.

"Different kinds of bear": Zhou lists *xiong* 熊 and *pi* 羆, both distinct but general terms for bear.

Water deer are Chinese water deer, *zhang* 獐. The same consideration applies to the word "cow" as mentioned earlier (note 73)—namely that it can refer to either a cow or a buffalo. The Chinese words I have translated as "leopards" and "goats" pose similar problems. *Bao* 豹 can mean either leopard or panther (*hei bao* 黑豹 "black leopard"), while *yang* 羊 can mean either sheep or goat (*shan yang* 山羊 "mountain sheep"). In her analysis of Khmer inscriptions, J. Jacob lists goats but not sheep, so I have opted for goats. However, she mentions neither leopards or panthers, so the choice in this case is more arbitrary. Jacob, "The Ecology of Angkor: Evidence from the Khmer Inscriptions," 293.

Another explanation for the special treatment of cows—in addition to the one in the second paragraph—could be the Hindu reverence for cows, still reflected today in the sacred cows of the royal palace in Phnom Penh.

Chapter 25: Vegetables

83. Winter gourds, also known as wax gourds, are large, fast-growing gourds that can be stored for months, hence their name. Snake gourds (*wang gua* 王瓜 or "king gourds" in Chinese) are a member of the cucumber family, with fruit that can grow up to two meters long and can be eaten like green beans. *Xian cai* 莧菜 can be identified with one or another type of amaranth, better known to us today as a flower than as a vegetable. CH, 1469; CMM, 33.

84. *Ku mai* 苦蕒, here translated "chicory," can be identified with chicory or endive. CMM, 229–230.

85. Silk cotton trees produce the kapok that Zhou mentions in chapter 11.

Chapter 26: Fish and Reptiles

86. Gudgeons or gobies (*tubu* 吐哺) are freshwater fish, usually quite small. They often swim close to the bottom of the river or lake, and this is said to account for a variant form of the fish's name, *tufu* 土附, "earth hugger." One version of the text (in *Gu jin tushu ji cheng* 古今圖書集成) drops the word for gudgeon, which makes some sense, in that carp can be large whereas gudgeon are usually not. XN, 156.

"Up to three pounds": Zhou writes "two *jin* or more." Two *jin* would be 2.75 pounds or 1.3 kilograms.

87. The Freshwater Sea is, again, the Tonle Sap Lake that Zhou mentions in the preface and in chapter 17.

88. There seem to be words missing before or after the references to eels, and I have added "There are also."

The sentence about soft-shell turtles and alligators is hard to understand. "As big as large pillars" is just a guess at the meaning for *da ru hezhu* 大如合苧, taking *hezhu* to be a homophone for *hezhu* 合柱, a hollow jointed pillar. Conceivably the phrase is a garbled version of a phrase that includes the term *he bao* 合抱, "judging a tree's size by joining your hands round it." Otherwise *hezhu* may be a Wenzhou dialect word, or the result of textual corruption.

The reference to "offal and all" is a means of translating the expression *liu cang zhi gui* 六藏之龜, "a turtle or tortoise with six internal organs" (taking 藏 as 臟). Zhou's expression here is odd, because by the standard Chinese reckoning of the time there were five internal organs—heart, liver, spleen, lungs, and kidney—rather than six (though the expression "six internal organs" did sometimes occur with the understanding that the two kidneys made up two organs rather than one). But in any case why describe the turtle this way? Perhaps it was just a way of saying "the whole turtle, offal and all." To this day tortoise meat and offal are regarded as a delicacy in Cambodian villages. Again, perhaps the text is corrupt. ZWD, vol. 4, 1464.

"Prawns from Zhanan weigh a pound and a half or more": Zhou writes: "one *jin* or more." As before, the inches are Chinese inches, a little longer than British and American inches.

Zhou apparently calls goose-necked barnacles by the name they are given in his home town Wenzhou, which is *gui jiao* 龜腳 or *gui zu* 龜足, "turtle foot." XN, 158; CH, 5169. Goose-necked barnacles, sometimes called goose barnacles, are crustacean delicacies in the form of barnacles anchored by a thick, flexible stalk that looks a little like a goose's head and neck.

In his general preface Zhou mentions Zhanan as being at the southern end of the Tonle Sap Lake. He also mentions Zhenpu in the preface as being on the southeast coast of Vietnam. He mentions Zhenpu again in chapter 18.

Chapter 27: Fermented Liquor

89. The leaf *pengyasi* 朋牙四 has not been identified with any degree of certainty. *Baolengjiao* 包稜角 [P *pawlengkjaw* K *pauliengkak*] may be the Cambodian words for cooked rice (*bai*) and husked rice (*ong-gor*), or more likely the word for husked rice with an unidentified first syllable. LRP, 29, 186, 152; GSR, 285, 239 (radicals with 夌), 314.

"... the leaves of a type of palm": Zhou writes of the leaves of a type of *jiao* 茭, usually a wild rice. But here *jiao* is generally taken to be a palm tree, perhaps the stemless nypa palm, whose leaves are sometimes called by the English name cadjan, from the Malay *kajang* for palm leaf. XN, 160; HJ, 139–140.

Chapter 28: Salt, Vinegar, and Soy Sauce

90. "No prohibition on salt works"—unlike in China, where salt manufacture was under strict government control, with salt manufacture authorized under license. On salt administration in Yuan China: CHC, 509, 511–512.

Bajian 巴澗 is not possible to locate, but must have been somewhere on the coast of the Mekong Delta. Zhenpu 真蒲 was the town Zhou mentions in the preface, and again in chapters 18 and 26.

91. Zhou transliterates a Khmer word that may be the word for tamarind, rather than writing the word for tamarind in Chinese. The transliteration is *xianping* 咸平 [P *xjamphing*, K *yamb'iwung*]; the Khmer word for tamarind is *om-bpeul*. LRP, 335, 240; GSR, 671, 825.

92. "A wine yeast": *jiu yao* 酒藥 (sometimes written 酒葯), a Chinese yeast for making wine that is usually a by-product of wine already made.

Chapter 29: Silk Production

93. Ramie is *zhu ma* 苧麻 in Chinese, its English name coming from the Malay *rami*. It is a tall plant that, like hemp, produces a strong fiber. It is not clear why Zhou mentions the fact that the Siamese have to do without ramie and hemp—perhaps the satiny silk *ling* 綾 that he refers to was blended with them, given that it is often blended. On the other hand the text here may be flawed: *zhu ma* is inverted as *ma zhu* 麻苧, while the character *zhu* 苧 has uncertain (dialect?) connotations, having been used oddly earlier, in the description of the size of alligators in chapter 26.

Chapter 30: Utensils

94. *Qia* 恰 has not been identified with a Khmer term with any certainty. The word Zhou uses for the item used to pour wine, *zhuzi* 注子, describes an old-

fashioned vessel, usually made of gold, bronze, or earthenware and shaped like a kettle.

95. Mingzhou 明州 was the town Zhou started from and returned to, as he mentions in the preface.

Chapter 31: Carts and Palanquins

96. Mentioned in chapter 4. Judging from reliefs at Bayon, the bend in the palanquin pole typically curved upward in the middle, rather than downward, so that the pole as a whole was shaped like a "W."

Chapter 32: Boats

97. The palm leaves are leaves from the nypa palm mentioned in chapter 27. The Cambodian words for *xinna* 新拿 and *pilan* 皮闌 have not been identified. XN speculates that *pilan* [P *phujlan*, K *b'jiclân*] may be related to *perahu*, the Malay word for boat, from which comes the English term prow (a small boat), or else to the South Indian word from which the archaic English term baloon (rowing vessel) is derived. XN, 171; HJ, 53, 733; LRP 236, 182.

Chapter 33: Prefectures

98. On the number of prefectures: different texts read "ninety or so" and "altogether ten or so" (*jiushi yu* 九十餘 and *fan shi yu* 凡十餘). Ten or so seems too few, given that Zhou lists ten and adds that he cannot record the names of the others. But ninety or so seems a large number, given Cambodia's size, even at the height of Yashodharapura's power—though as mentioned earlier much depends on the size of the administrative unit Zhou calls *jun* or prefecture. By way of comparison, the number of prefectures in the whole of China under the Mongols was 217.

Some though not all of the places Zhou names can be tentatively identified or located on the map. Zhenpu, Zhanan, and Bijian have already been discussed (notes 2, 4, and 90). Baxue 八薛 [P Pasje, K Pasiät] may be Pakse in southern Laos, which is near a temple built by Jayavarman IV, king of Angkor in the tenth century. Pumai 蒲買 seems to be Phimai, the walled temple complex south of the modern Thai city of Nakhon Ratchasima, which was a center of Cambodian royal patronage for part of the twelfth and thirteenth century. Zhigun 雉棍 may be Saigon, now Ho Chi Minh City in southern Vietnam. Moliang 莫良, Laigankeng 賴敢坑, and Basili 八廝里 have not been clearly identified, though it has been suggested that Moliang could be Pailin, the gem-rich region near the border between Cambodia and Thailand. XN, 173; Smithies, *The Customs of Cambodia*, 87; www.phimai.ca; LRP, 27, 351; GSR, 29, 89.

"Their officials": the phrase in Chinese, *guan shu* 官屬, can mean officials and their subordinates. The same term *shu* 屬 is used in the title of the chapter, *shu jun* 屬郡, which strictly speaking refers to prefectures subordinate to, or belonging to, the Cambodian state.

Chapter 34: Villages

99. "... Buddhist temple or pagoda": The precise connotation of *ta* 塔, which I have taken to mean pagoda, is uncertain here; it may mean tower rather than pagoda, in which case it would refer to non-Buddhist structures of some kind. As it stands this sentence cannot, therefore, be taken (as some have taken it) to mean definitively that Buddhism was paramount in villages. *Maijie* 買節 [P *majtsje*, K *maitsiet*] may correspond to the Khmer *mai s'rok*, headman of a village or district, though the correspondence with *s'rok* is not convincing. One of several possible explanations of the term *senmu* 森木 [P *semmu*, K *siemmuk*] is that it is the Khmer word *som-raak*, to rest or stay in a guesthouse. LRP, 206, 155, 273, 220; GSR, 317, 113, 176, 312.

Stele inscriptions tell of the importance to Cambodia at this time of rest houses, which were built by Jayavarman VII along the main roads between the capital and other locations, including Champa and Phimai, the latter being one of the prefectures mentioned in chapter 33. On the road to Champa there were at one time fifty-seven rest houses located at regular intervals. The stone remains of some rest houses are still standing. The Chinese postal stations to which Zhou compares these resting-houses were an equally important element of the Chinese state, and were rapidly developed during Yuan times. By the time Khubilai Khan died the country had more than 1,400 postal stations set at regular intervals along main roads and serviced by about 50,000 horses. Marco Polo was among the foreign visitors who praised their efficiency. Chandler, *A History of Cambodia*, 61–62; Rossabi, *Khubilai Khan*, 124; Latham, *Marco Polo: The Travels*, 150–155.

The tantalizingly brief reference to recent wars or battles with the Siamese— Zhou uses the term *jiao bing* 交兵, a joining of soldiers, which may refer to either a battle or a war, and the word *lü* 屢 "repeatedly" indicates that there was more than one such event—raises important questions about the security of late thirteenth-century Cambodia that Zhou leaves unanswered.

Chapter 35: Taking Gall

100. It seems that the Chams—like the Chinese and the Europeans— regarded gall as a source of bravery and courage. *Ming shi* 明史 also tells how the Chams themselves collected gall from unwitting travelers for the king of Champa, who drank it and even bathed in it so that "his body was permeated by it." The only difference was that according to *Ming shi*, gall from Chinese was prized above all others, the opposite of the Cambodian view reported by Zhou. In an account of his travels in Indochina in the mid-nineteenth century, the French priest Charles Emile Bouillevaux wrote that the custom of stealing gall persisted even then. On the Cham king bathing in gall: *Ming shi*, juan 324, 8392–8393. On Bouillevaux: XN, 177–178. The *Ming shi* account is given in English in G. Wade, *The Ming shi Account of Champa* (Singapore, June 2003), 19.

Chapter 36: A Strange Affair

101. "A barbarian": *man* 蠻, "a southern barbarian," meaning a Cambodian.

102. "... lived in this place": Literally, "lived in the foreign place," following the Ming *Shuo fu* variant *fan di ju* 番地居. XN, 178.

"... fellow countryman": Zhou writes that Xue 薛 is his *xiang ren* 鄉人, meaning that he comes from Wenzhou or thereabouts, rather than just anywhere in China. We know nothing else about this man.

Chapter 37: Bathing

103. "... fifth watch": Refers to the last watch or division of the night by Chinese reckoning, since, as Zhou told us in chapter 13, the Cambodians had only four watches.

Chapter 39: The Army

104. In this passage Zhou uses the same term for missile-throwing engine or trebuchet, *pao* 砲, as he does in his description of the fireworks on New Year's Day in chapter 13 (see note 59). Here it is in the term *pao shi* 砲石, which means literally "trebuchets and rocks" and by customary inversion "rock-throwing trebuchets."

Chapter 40: The King in and Out of the Palace

105. The old king was Jayavarman VIII. His replacement Indravarman III, who reigned from 1296 to 1308, was the king Zhou saw and describes here and in chapter 6.

106. *Cu* 殂 "died" is a variant, from the second, Qing edition of *Shuo fu*. Other versions of the text give *ai nü* 愛女 "loved his daughter" instead of *cu*, so that it reads: "His wife's father loved his daughter, and she secretly stole... ." *Cu* seems marginally more plausible, since if the old man had loved his daughter so much she would have had no need of stealth.

107. It is not clear whether the dignitaries and royal relatives were in front of the whole procession, or in front of the king and behind the soldiers. The procession of Suryavarman II that is shown on a relief in Angkor Wat, the only known portrait of a royal procession at Angkor, depicts the king surrounded by his army, with soldiers taking up the whole of the front part of the procession.

108. "He only used a gold chariot... .": This sentence was originally part of the description of the royal audience later in this chapter, where it was out of place. I

have moved it forward so that it complements the sentence before it by describing the king's means of transport for both long and short journeys.

109. The Chinese term *sanba* 三罷 is a transliteration of the Cambodian word *som-pee-ah*, the term for the gesture described.

110. In Chinese the precise meaning of the phrase "without anything fixed in writing," *wu ding wen* 無定文, is unclear. Literally meaning "without fixed writings," it may mean that the king's pronouncements are made without prior agenda or documentation, or without being noted down as they are made, or both.

111. Zhou here uses the broader term *man mo* 蠻貃 for barbarians, *mo* 貃 being another word used both generically for outsiders and specifically for certain tribes called Mo [p Maj, k Muk] in both North and South China and beyond. On the Mo, see Schafer, *The Vermilion Bird*, 50–53 (where Schafer calls them Mak); also CH, 5167; LRP, 218; GSR, 206.

APPENDIX I

OTHER EARLY ACCOUNTS OF CAMBODIA IN CHINESE

EVEN IN ITS present incomplete form, Zhou Daguan's account of the civilization of Angkor is unique in its length, breadth, and detail. But it is not the only early Chinese account of Cambodia. For a thousand years before Zhou was born, Chinese historians and annalists included entries on Zhenla and Funan (the very earliest name associated with Cambodia) in many of their writings. Moreover, in several cases the subject matter of their accounts of the country was quite similar to the subject matter in Zhou's book. So was the order it is presented in.

From one point of view this is a bit of a disappointment. It detracts from our sense that Zhou was writing his own book in his own fashion. But it is good to bear in mind that early literary Chinese writings about exotic lands tended to be somewhat formulaic. Typically, for any given country a brief description was given of the place's history and its dealings with the Chinese imperial court. In addition, there was a short, usually dry, account of the appearance, habits, and beliefs of its people, and a list or lists of its main products. On occasion the writer would recount unusual or bizarre phenomena (like the accounts of trial by ordeal to be found in several early texts on Cambodia, or Zhou Daguan's own account of the *zhentan* ritual for young girls).

Broadly speaking Zhou Daguan conformed to this approach, sometimes quite mechanically—for example, in his lists of native animals, birds, trees, plants, and products—but frequently in a less humdrum way by describing things in much more detail and more personally than was usually the case. Old Chinese writings about strange lands thus gave Zhou a genre model, a kind of template, but one that he used and developed in his own particular, sometimes idiosyncratic, manner.

In their valuable compilation of materials from old Chinese books relating to Cambodia,[1] the Chinese scholars Lu Junling and Zhou Shaoquan list accounts of, or references to, Funan and Zhenla in over seventy sources (including Zhou Daguan's book) up to and including the Yuan dynasty. The first of these is the third-century history *Annals of the Three Kingdoms* (*San guo zhi* 三國志), which refers to Funan twice, but only in passing. The first account of any substance is the description of Zhenla in the seventh-century official *History of the Sui Dynasty* (*Sui shu* 隋書).

The account in this early official history starts to bring old Cambodia to life. It mentions the capital with its "twenty thousand or so families" and its "large hall where the king listens to affairs of state" once every three days, as well as the thirty other cities with their several thousand families that make up the realm. It includes a description of the king's dress and jewels, and transliterations of the Khmer names of five ranks of officials, as well as a portrait of how officials knelt around the king before and after audiences with him. It also describes the animal sacrifices the king performed in the fifth and sixth months of the year so as to dispel "noxious vapors."

In a phrase that is to recur in several subsequent texts, and which Zhou echoes in chapter six of his book, the *History of the Sui Dynasty* describes the people as "small in stature and black in color, with some among the women white." It recounts the people's washing habits, their food and eating habits, their marriages and their funeral rites, and notes the presence of Buddhist monks and monks that (like Zhou) it calls "Daoist." It also lists a number of exotic trees and plants, and comments on the sea fish that spout water and have noses like elephants, as well as the lake fish "that look like a mountain when they are half out of the water."

There is almost exactly the same account of the king's mid-year sacrifices in the official *Old History of the Tang Dynasty* (*Jiu Tang shu* 舊唐書), which also gives a somewhat cursory account of the country and its people. The official *New History of the Tang Dynasty* (*Xin Tang shu* 新唐書), completed in 1060, a century or so after the *Old History of the Tang Dynasty*, carries a comparable but even briefer account. The references to Zhenla in the next official history of substance, *History of the Song Dynasty* (*Song shi* 宋史) are equally summary.

There is a somewhat longer description of Zhenla in the much-used eleventh-century geographical compendium *Record of the World of Great Peace* (*Taiping huanyu ji* 太平寰宇記), but it seems to be drawn from earlier accounts, particularly the account in the *History of the Sui Dynasty*, some of which it repeats word for word.

Two fuller accounts of Cambodia were current when Zhou was alive and must have been well known to him. These are the descriptions of Zhenla in the thirteenth-century *Treatise on the Various Foreigners* (*Zhu fan zhi* 諸蕃志), and in the fourteenth-century *Comprehensive Assessment of Historical Records* (*Wen xian tong kao* 文獻通考). We know Zhou was familiar with the *Treatise on the Various Foreigners* because he mentions it in his preface.[2] This book repeats some earlier materials but adds new materials of its own. These include descriptions of the king's palace, with its grand chambers and gold bridges spanning lotus ponds, and of the bronze tower to the southwest, with its bronze towers and eight heavy bronze elephants. It also mentions three hundred dancing girls responsible for offering food to the devoutly worshipped Buddha, and notes the fine chanting of the Buddhist monks, who it says were divided between those with families, dressed in yellow, and those in the pagodas, dressed in red. Like the *History of the Sui Dynasty*, it mentions

Daoists and reports that they wore leaves from trees. After listing the country's products the *Treatise on the Various Foreigners* concludes by listing the names of thirteen "states" subordinate to Zhenla, a kind of precursor to chapter 33 of Zhou Daguan's work.

The second of the two books, *Comprehensive Assessment of Historical Records*, came into circulation around 1307, so it would have been current at about the time Zhou got back to Wenzhou from his travels. Its author Ma Duanlin 馬端臨 was a renowned scholar from Raozhou 饒州 in Southeast China, not so veryfar from Wenzhou. The book's relatively long section on Cambodia reproduces many of the stories and even the phrases of earlier accounts, including the comment that "the people are small in stature and black in color, with some among the women white." But there is no sign that Ma Duanlin knew anything about Zhou's journey or had read any account of it. Perhaps this is further evidence that Zhou did not write his book as soon as he returned, but rather sometime later in life.

NOTES

1. Lu Junling 陸峻岭 and Zhou Shaoquan 周紹泉, ed. *Zhongguo guji zhong you guan jianpuzhai ziliao huibian* 中國古籍中有關柬埔寨資料匯編 (*Collection of Materials on Cambodia in Old Chinese Books*, Beijing: Zhonghua shuju, 1986).

2. I also quote from it in notes 5 and 13.

APPENDIX II

CHINESE DYNASTIES, MONGOL EMPERORS OF CHINA, AND CAMBODIAN KINGS

Chinese dynasties

1600?– ?1046 BCE	Shang
1046?–221 BCE	Zhou
221–206 BCE	Qin
202 BCE–220 CE	Han
581–618	Sui
618–907	Tang
960–1279	Song
1279–1368	Yuan (Mongols)
1368–1644	Ming
1644–1911	Qing (Manchus)

First five Yuan emperors (with imperial names)

1279–1294	Khubilai Khan (Shizu)
1294–1307	Temür (Chengzong)
1307–1311	Khaishan (Wuzong)
1311–1320	Ayurbarwada (Renzong)
1321–1323	Shidebala (Yingzong)

Cambodian kings at Angkor, 13th to early 14th centuries

1181–?1220	Jayavarman vii
1220–1243 or 1270	Indravarman ii
1243 or 1270–1295	Jayavarman viii
1295–1307	Indravarman iii
1307–1327	Indrajayavarman

WORKS CONSULTED

Abbreviations

CH   *Ci hai* 辭海. Shanghai: Shanghai cishu chuanbanshe, 1989.

CHC   Franke, Herbert, and Denis Twitchett, ed. *The Cambridge History of China: Volume 6, Alien Regimes and Border States, 907–1368.* Cambridge: Cambridge University Press, 1994.

CHM   Wilkinson, Endymion. *Chinese History: A Manual (Revised and Enlarged).* Cambridge and London: Harvard University Asia Center, 2000.

CMM   Stuart, G. A. *Chinese Materia Medica: Vegetable Kingdom.* Taipei Southern Materials Center, 1987.

GSR   Karlgren, Bernard. *Grammata Serica Recensa.* Stockholm: Museum of Far Eastern Antiquities, 1964.

HJ   Yule, Henry, and A. C. Burnell. *Hobson-Jobson: A Glossary of Colloquial Anglo-Indian Words and Phrases.* New Delhi: Munshiram Manoharlal, 1984.

LRP   Pulleyblank, Edwin G. *Lexicon of Reconstructed Pronunciation in Early Middle Chinese, Late Middle Chinese, and Early Mandarin.* Vancouver: UBC Press, 1991.

PP   Pelliot, Paul. *Mémoires sur les Coutumes du Cambodge de Tcheou Ta-kouan.* Paris: Adrien Maisonneuve, 1997.

XN   Xia Nai 夏鼐 et al., ed. *Zhenla fengtu ji jiao zhu, Xi you lu, Yi yü zhi* 真臘風土記校注，西遊錄，異域志. Beijing: Zhonghua shuju, 2000.

ZWD   *Zhongwen da cidian* 中文大辭典. Taipei: Zhongguo wenhua xueyuan, 1968.

Allsen, Thomas. "The Rise of the Mongolian Empire and Mongolian Rule in North China." In *The Cambridge History of China: Volume 6, Alien Regimes and Border States, 907–1368*, edited by H. Franke and D. Twitchett. Cambridge: Cambridge University Press, 1994.

Balazs, Etienne. *Chinese Civilization and Bureaucracy*, translated by H. M. Wright. New Haven and London: Yale University Press, 1964.

Briggs, L. P. *The Ancient Khmer Empire*. Philadelphia: American Philosophical Society, 1951.

Cambodia Country Map. Singapore: Periplus Editions, 2004(?).

Chan, Elisabeth. *Tropical Plants of Indonesia*. Singapore: Periplus, 1998.

Chandler, David. *A History of Cambodia*. Boulder and Oxford: Westview Press, 2000.

———. "The Legend of the Leper King (1978)." In *Facing the Cambodian Past*. Chiang Mai: Silkworm Books, 1996.

———. *Facing the Cambodian Past*. Chiang Mai: Silkworm Books, 1996.

Chen Zhengxiang 陳正祥. *Zhenla fengtu ji yanjiu* 真臘風土記研究 [*Research on 'Cambodia: The Land and its People'*]. Hong Kong: Xianggang zhongwen daxue chuban, 1975.

Ci hai 辭海 [*Sea of Words*]. Shanghai: Shanghai cishu chubanshe, 1989.

Clark, Joyce, ed. *Bayon: New Perspectives*. Bangkok: River Books, 2007.

Coedès, Georges. "Notes sur Tcheou Ta-kouan" ["Notes on Zhou Daguan"]. *Bulletin de l'cole Française d'Extrême Orient*, Vol. 18 (no. 9), 1921.

———. "Nouvelles Notes sur Tcheou Ta-kouan" ["New Notes on Zhou Daguan"]. *T'oung Pao*, Series ii, Vol. 30, 1933.

———. *The Indianized States of Southeast Asia*, translated by S. Cowing. Honolulu: University of Hawaii Press, 1996.

d'Arcy Paul, J. Gilman, tr. *The Customs of Cambodia by Chou Ta-kuan (Zhou Daguan)*. Bangkok: The Siam Society, 1993.

Da Tang xi yu ji 大唐西域記 [*Great Tang Dynasty Record of the Western Regions*]. Beijing: Zhonghua shuju, 1985.

Dikötter, Frank. *The Discourse of Race in Modern China*. London: Hurst & Co, 1992.

Dubs, Homer H., tr. and ed. *The History of the Former Han Dynasty*. Baltimore: Waverley Press, 1938.

Fitzgerald, C. P. *The Southern Expansion of the Chinese People*. Bangkok: White Lotus, 1993.

Franke, Herbert, and Denis Twitchett, ed. *The Cambridge History of China: Volume 6, Alien Regimes and Border States, 907–1368*. Cambridge: Cambridge University Press, 1994.

Freeman, Michael, and Claude Jacques. *Ancient Angkor*. Bangkok: River Books, 2003.

Gernet, Jacques. *Daily Life in China on the Eve of the Mongol Invasion 1250–1276*. London: George Allen and Unwin, 1962.

Gernet, Jacques. *A History of Chinese Civilization*. Cambridge: Cambridge University Press, 1996.

Gibb, H. A. R., tr. and ed. *Ibn Battuta: Travels in Asia and Africa, 1325–1354*. Delhi: LPP, 1999.

Glaize, Maurice. *Les Monuments du Groupe d'Angkor* [*The Angkor Group of Monuments*]. Paris: J. Maisonneuve, 2003.

Groslier, Bernard. *Indochina*. London: Barrie and Jenkins, 1970.

Hanyu da cidian 漢語大詞典 [*A Large Dictionary of Chinese*]. Shanghai: Hanyu da cidian chubanshe, 1986–1994.

Harris, Peter, ed. *The Travels of Marco Polo*. New York and London: Alfred A. Knopf Everyman Library, 2008.

Higham, Charles. *The Civilization of Angkor*. Berkeley and Los Angeles: University of California Press, 2001.

Hong Ye 洪業 et al., ed. *Liao Jin zhuan ji zonghe yinde* 寮金元傳記三十種綜合得 [*A Comprehensive Index of Thirty Biographical Records of the Liao, Jin, and Yuan Dynasties*] Beijing: Harvard-Yenching Institute, 1940.

Hsiao Ch'i-ch'ing. "Mid-Yüan politics." In *The Cambridge History of China: Volume 6, Alien Regimes and Border States, 907–1368*, edited by H. Franke and D. Twitchett. Cambridge: Cambridge University Press, 1994.

Huai nanzi yi zhu 准南子譯注 [*Huai nanzi with Translation and Notes*]. Jilin: Jilin wenshi chubanshe, 1990.

Hucker, Charles. *A Dictionary of Official Titles in Imperial China*. Stanford: Stanford University Press, 1985.

Hudson, Geoffrey. *Europe and China*. London: Edward Arnold, 1931.

Jacob, Judith. *Cambodian Linguistics, Literature and History*. London: School of Oriental and African Studies, 1993.

———. "The Ecology of Angkor: Evidence from the Khmer Inscriptions." In *Cambodian Linguistics, Literature and History*. London: School of Oriental and African Studies, 1993.

Jacques, Claude. *Angkor*. Köln: Könemann, 1999.

———. "'Funan', 'Zhenla': The Reality Concealed by these Chinese Views of Indochina." In *Early South East Asia: Essays in Archaeology, History, and Historical Geography*, edited by R. B. Smith and W. Watson. New York: Oxford University Press, 1979.

Jessup, Helen Ibbitson. *Art and Architecture of Cambodia*. London: Thames and Hudson, 2004.

Karlgren, Bernhard. *Grammata Serica Recensa*. Stockholm: Museum of Far Eastern Antiquities, 1964.

Larner, John. *Marco Polo and the Discovery of the World*. New Haven and London: Yale University Press, 1999.

Latham, Ronald, tr. and ed. *Marco Polo: The Travels*. London: Penguin Books, 1958.

Li Chongxing 李崇興. *Yuan yuyan cidian* 元語言詞典 [*Yuan Language Dictionary*]. Shanghai: Shanghai jiaoyu chubanshe, 1998.

Lu Junling 陸峻岭 and Zhou Shaoquan 周紹泉, ed. *Zhongguo guji zhong you guan jianpuzhai ziliao huibian* 中國古籍中有關柬埔寨資料匯編 [*Collection of Materials on Cambodia in Old Chinese Books*]. Beijing: Zhonghua shuju, 1986.

Mackerras, Colin. *Chinese Drama: A Historical Survey*. Beijing: New World Press, 1990.

McGregor, R. S. *The Oxford Hindi-English Dictionary*. Delhi: Oxford University Press, 1993.

Ming shi 明史 [*History of the Ming Dynasty*]. Beijing: Zhonghua shuju, 1974.

Monier-Williams, Monier. *English-Sanskrit Dictionary*. Delhi Munshiram Manoharlal, 1995.

Mote, F. W. *Imperial China, 900–1800*. Cambridge: Harvard University Press, 1999.

———. "Confucian Eremitism in the Yuan Period." In *The Confucian Persuasion*, edited by Arthur Wright. Stanford: Stanford University Press, 1960.

———. "Chinese Society under Mongol Rule, 1215–1368." In *The Cambridge History of China: Volume 6, Alien Regimes and Border States, 907–1368*, edited by H. Franke and D. Twitchett. Cambridge: Cambridge University Press, 1994.

Needham, Joseph. *Science and Civilization in China, Volume 3: Mathematics and the Sciences of the Heavens and the Earth*. Cambridge: Cambridge University Press, 1959.

———. *Science and Civilization in China, Volume 4: Physics and Physical Technology, Part I*. Cambridge: Cambridge University Press, 1962.

———. *Science and Civilization in China, Volume 4, Physics and Physical Technology, Part III*. Cambridge: Cambridge University Press, 1971.

———. *Science and Civilization in China, Volume 5, 3: Chemistry and Chemical Technology, Part III*. Cambridge: Cambridge University Press, 1976.

———. *Science and Civilization in China, Volume 5, 7: Chemistry and Chemical Technology, Part 7*. Cambridge: Cambridge University Press, 1986.

Nienhauser, William, Jr., ed. *The Indiana Companion to Traditional Chinese Literature, Volume 1*. Bloomington and Indianapolis: Indiana University Press, 1986.

Pelliot, Paul, tr. and ed. *Mémoires sur les Coutumes du Cambodge de Tcheou Ta-kouan [Zhou Daguan's Memoirs on the Customs of Cambodia]*. Paris: Adrien Maisonneuve, 1997.

Pulleyblank, Edwin G. *Lexicon of Reconstructed Pronunciation in Early Middle Chinese, Late Middle Chinese, and Early Mandarin*. Vancouver: ubc Press, 1991.

Rachewiltz, Igor de, and Miyoko Nakano. *Index to Biographical Material in Chin and Yuan Literary Works, First Series*. Canberra: Australian National University Press, 1970.

Rachewiltz, Igor de, and May Wang. *Index to Biographical Material in Chin and Yuan Literary Works, Second Series*. Canberra: Australian National University Press, 1972.

————. *Repertory of Proper Names in Yüan Literary Sources*. Taipei: Southern Materials Center, Inc, 1988.

Reid, Anthony. *Charting the Shape of Early Modern Southeast Asia*. Chiangmai: Silkworm Books, 1999.

Reid, Anthony, ed. *Sojourners and Settlers: Histories of Southeast Asia and the Chinese*. Honolulu: University of Hawai'i Press, 1996.

Ren Jiyu 任繼愈, ed. *Fojiao da cidian* 佛教大辭典 [*A Large Dictionary of Buddhism*]. Shanghai: Jiangsu guji chubanshe, 2002.

Rooney, Dawn. *Angkor: An Introduction to the Temples*. New York: W. W. Norton, 2004.

Rossabi, Morris. *Khubilai Khan, His Life and Times*. Berkeley, Los Angeles, and London: University of California Press, 1988.

————. "The Reign of Khubilai khan." In *The Cambridge History of China: Volume 6, Alien Regimes and Border States, 907–1368*, edited by H. Franke and D. Twitchett. Cambridge: Cambridge University Press, 1994.

Sahai, Sachchidanand. *Les Institutions Politiques et l'Organisation Administrative du Cambodge Ancien (vie-xiiie Siècles)* [*The Political Institutions and Administrative Organization of Ancient Cambodia (6th to 13th Centuries)*]. Paris, École Française d'Extrême Orient, 1970.

Schafer, Edward. *The Vermilion Bird: Tang Images of the South*. Berkeley and Los Angeles: University of California Press, 1967.

Smith, R. B., and William Watson, ed. *Early South East Asia: Essays in Archaeology, History, and Historical Geography*. New York: Oxford University Press, 1979.

Smithies, Michael, tr. and ed. *The Customs of Cambodia by Zhou Daguan (Chou Takuan)*. Bangkok: The Siam Society, 2001.

Smyth, David, and Tran Kien. *Practical Cambodian Dictionary*. Rutland and Tokyo: Charles E Tuttle, 1995.

Song shi 宋史 [*History of the Song Dynasty*]. Beijing and Shanghai: Zhonghua shuju, 1977.

Stuart, G. A. *Chinese Materia Medica: Vegetable Kingdom.* Taipei: Southern Materials Center, 1987.

Stuart-Fox, Martin. *A Short History of China and Southeast Asia: Tribute, Trade and Influence.* Crows Nest, New South Wales: Allen and Unwin, 2003.

Tillman, Hoyt. *Confucian Discourse and Chu Hsi's Ascendancy.* Honolulu: University of Hawai'i Press, 1992.

Trainor, Kevin, ed. *Buddhism: The Illustrated Guide.* New York: Oxford University Press, 2001.

Vickery, Michael. *Society, Economics and Politics in Pre-Angkor Cambodia: The 7th–8th Centuries.* Tokyo: Toyo Bunko, 1998.

Wade, Geoff. *The Ming shi Account of Champa.* Singapore: National University of Singapore, Asia Research Institute Working Paper, June 2003.

Walravens, Hartmut. *Paul Pelliot (1878–1945): His Life and Works—A Bibliography.* Bloomington: Indiana University Research Institute for Inner Asian Studies, 2001.

Wang Gungwu. *The Chinese Overseas: From Earthbound China to the Quest for Autonomy.* Cambridge and London: Harvard University Press, 2000.

Watters, Thomas. *On Yuan Chwang's Travels in India.* Delhi: Munshiram Manoharlal, 1973.

Wilkinson, Endymion. *Chinese History: A Manual (Revised and Enlarged).* Cambridge and London: Harvard University Asia Center, 2000.

Wood, F. *Did Marco Polo Go to China?* (Boulder: Westview Press, 1996).

Xia Nai 夏鼐 et al., ed. *Zhenla fengtu ji jiao zhu, Xi you lu, Yi yu zhi* 真臘風土記校注，西遊錄，異域志 [*Cambodia: The Land and Its People, annotated edition; A Record of a Journey to the West; A Treatise on Strange Frontier Lands*]. Beijing: Zhonghua shuju, 2000.

Xu Xiqi 徐錫棋, ed. *Xin bian Zhongguo san qian nian li ri jiansuo biao* 新編中國三千年歷日檢索表 [*Newly Compiled Search Table for Chinese Calendar Days for 3000 Years*]. Beijing: Renmin jiaoyu chubanshe, 1992.

Yuan shi 元史 [*History of the Yuan Dynasty*]. Beijing and Shanghai: Zhonghua shuju, 1976.

Yule, Henry, ed. *The Travels of Marco Polo: the Complete Yule-Cordier Edition.* New York: Dover Publications, 1993.

Yule, Henry, and A. C. Burnell. *Hobson-Jobson: A Glossary of Colloquial Anglo-Indian Words and Phrases.* New Delhi: Munshiram Manoharlal, 1984.

Yung Wai-chuen, Peter. *Angkor: The Khmers in Ancient Chinese Annals.* Hong Kong: Oxford University Press, 2000.

Zhang Peiheng and Luo Yuming. *Zhongguo wenxue shi* 中國文學史 [*History of Chinese Literature*]. Shanghai: Fudan daxue chubanshe, 1996.

Zhonghua renmin gongheguo fen sheng ditu ji 中華人民共和國分省地圖集 [*Provincial Atlas of the Chinese People's Republic*]. Beijing: Ditu chubanshe, n.d.

Zhongwen da cidian 中文大辭典 [*A Large Dictionary of Chinese*]. Taipei: Zhongguo wenhua xueyuan, 1968.

INDEX

Zhou Daguan is referred to as Zhou, and *A Record of Cambodia–The Land and Its People* is referred to as *Record*. References to the text of *Record* are given in bold.